CONTENTS

INTRODUCTION

Cooking your food using all-natural methods is becoming a trendy revival these days. Gone are the days when people would want to cook their food using their microwave ovens. And with people finding more time to experiment in the kitchen, many try cooking methods that they would not normally use such as grilling and smoking. Many people experiment on these cooking methods not only because they have a lot of time to do kitchen experiments in their homes but the closure of their favorite restaurants meant that they are no longer able to enjoy their favorite restaurant-quality barbecue and smoked meats. So instead of just dreaming of the day when you can finally eat restaurant-caliber smoked barbecue, now is the time for you to go and get yourself a grill particularly the Traeger Grill. And let this book serve as your ultimate guide to using your Traeger Grill and cooking sumptuous grilled foods cooked at the comfort of your home.

RED MEAT RECIPES

PERFECT BEEF TENDERLOIN

Serves: 12 | **Cooking Time:** 1 hour 19 mins | **Prep Time:** 10 mins

INGREDIENTS:

- 1 (5-lb.) beef tenderloin, trimmed
- Kosher salt, to taste
- ¼ C. olive oil
- Freshly ground black pepper, to taste

INSTRUCTIONS:

1. With kitchen strings, tie the tenderloin at 7-8 places.
2. Season tenderloin with kosher salt generously.
3. With a plastic wrap, cover the tenderloin and set aside at room temperature for about 1 hour.
4. Set the temperature of Traeger Grill to 225-250 degrees F and preheat with closed lid for 15 mins.
5. Now, coat tenderloin with oil evenly and season with black pepper.
6. Arrange tenderloin onto the grill and cook for about 55-65 mins.
7. Now, place cooking grate directly over hot coals and sear tenderloin for about 2 mins per side.
8. Remove the tenderloin from grill and place onto a cutting board for about 10-15 mins before serving.
9. With a sharp knife, cut the tenderloin into desired-sized slices and serve.

NUTRITION INFORMATION:

Calories per serving: 425; Carbohydrates:
0g; Protein: 54.7g; Fat: 21.5g; Sugar: 0g;
Sodium: 123mg; Fiber: 0g

VERSATILE BEEF TENDERLOIN

Serves: 6 | **Cooking Time:** 2 hours 5 mins | **Prep Time:** 15 mins

INGREDIENTS:

For Brandy Butter:
- ½ C. butter
- 1 oz. brandy

For Brandy Sauce:
- 2 oz. brandy
- 8 garlic cloves, minced
- ¼ C. mixed fresh herbs (parsley, rosemary and thyme), chopped
- 2 tsp. honey
- 2 tsp. hot English mustard

For Tenderloin:
- 1 (2-lb.) center-cut beef tenderloin
- Salt and cracked black peppercorns, to taste

INSTRUCTIONS:

1. Set the temperature of Traeger Grill to 230 degrees F and preheat with closed lid for 15 mins.
2. For brandy butter: in a pan, melt butter over medium-low heat.
3. Stir in brandy and remove from heat.
4. Set aside, covered to keep warm.
5. For brandy sauce: in a bowl, add all ingredients and mix until well combined.
6. Season the tenderloin with salt and black peppercorns generously.
7. Coat tenderloin with brandy sauce evenly.
8. With a baster-injector, inject tenderloin with brandy butter.
9. Place the tenderloin onto the grill and cook for about 1½-2 hours, injecting with brandy butter occasionally.
10. Remove the tenderloin from grill and place onto a cutting board for about 10-15 mins before serving.
11. With a sharp knife, cut the tenderloin into desired-sized slices and serve.

NUTRITION INFORMATION:

Calories per serving: 496; Carbohydrates: 4.4g; Protein: 44.4g; Fat: 29.3g; Sugar: 2g; Sodium: 240mg; Fiber: 0.7g

BUTTERED TENDERLOIN

Serves: 8 | **Cooking Time:** 45 mins | **Prep Time:** 10 mins

INGREDIENTS:

- 1 (4-lb.) beef tenderloin, trimmed
- Smoked salt and cracked black pepper, to taste
- 3 tbsp. butter, melted

INSTRUCTIONS:

1. Set the temperature of Traeger Grill to 300 degrees F and preheat with closed lid for 15 mins.
2. Season the tenderloin with salt and black pepper generously and then rub with butter.
3. Place the tenderloin onto the grill and cook for about 45 mins.
4. Remove the tenderloin from grill and place onto a cutting board for about 10-15 mins before serving.
5. With a sharp knife, cut the tenderloin into desired-sized slices and serve.

NUTRITION INFORMATION:

Calories per serving: 505; Carbohydrates: 0g; Protein: 65.7g; Fat: 25.1g; Sugar: 0g; Sodium: 184mg; Fiber: 0g

DELISH BEEF BRISKET

Serves: 10 | **Cooking Time:** 7 hours | **Prep Time:** 10 mins

INGREDIENTS:

- 1 C. paprika
- ¾ C. sugar
- 3 tbsp. garlic salt
- 3 tbsp. onion powder
- 1 tbsp. celery salt
- 1 tbsp. lemon pepper
- 1 tbsp. ground black pepper
- 1 tsp. cayenne pepper
- 1 tsp. mustard powder
- ½ tsp. dried thyme, crushed
- 1 (5-6-lb.) beef brisket, trimmed

INSTRUCTIONS:

1. In a bowl, place all ingredients except for beef brisket and mix well.
2. Rub the brisket with spice mixture generously.
3. With a plastic wrap, cover the brisket and refrigerate overnight.
4. Set the temperature of Traeger Grill to 250 degrees F and preheat with closed lid for 15 mins.
5. Place the brisket onto grill over indirect heat and cook for about 3-3½ hours.
6. Flip and cook for about 3-3½ hours more.
7. Remove the brisket from grill and place onto a cutting board for about 10-15 mins before slicing.
8. With a sharp knife, cut the brisket in desired sized slices and serve.

NUTRITION INFORMATION:

Calories per serving: 536; Carbohydrates: 24.8g; Protein: 71.1g; Fat: 15.6g; Sugar: 17.4g; Sodium: 158mg; Fiber: 4.5g

ST. PATRICK DAY'S CORNED BEEF

Serves: 14 | **Cooking Time:** 7 hours | **Prep Time:** 15 mins

INGREDIENTS:

- 6 lb. corned beef brisket, drained, rinsed and pat dried
- Freshly ground black pepper, to taste
- 8 oz. light beer

INSTRUCTIONS:

1. Set the temperature of Traeger Grill to 275 degrees F and preheat with closed lid for 15 mins.
2. Sprinkle the beef brisket with spice packet evenly.
3. Now, sprinkle the brisket with black pepper lightly.
4. Place the brisket onto the grill and cook for about 3-4 hours.
5. Remove from grill and transfer briskets into an aluminum pan.
6. Add enough beer just to cover the bottom of pan.
7. With a piece of foil, cover the pan, leaving one corner open to let out steam.
8. Cook for about 2-3 hours.
9. Remove the brisket from grill and place onto a cutting board for about 10-15 mins before slicing.
10. With a sharp knife, cut the brisket in desired sized slices and serve.
11. Remove the brisket from grill and place onto a cutting board for about 25-30 mins before slicing.
12. With a sharp knife, cut the brisket in desired sized slices and serve.

NUTRITION INFORMATION:

Calories per serving: 337; Carbohydrates: 0.6g; Protein: 26.1g; Fat: 24.3g; Sugar: 0g; Sodium: 1719mg; Fiber: 0g

SPICED RUMP ROAST

Serves: 8 | **Cooking Time:** 6 hours | **Prep Time:** 10 mins

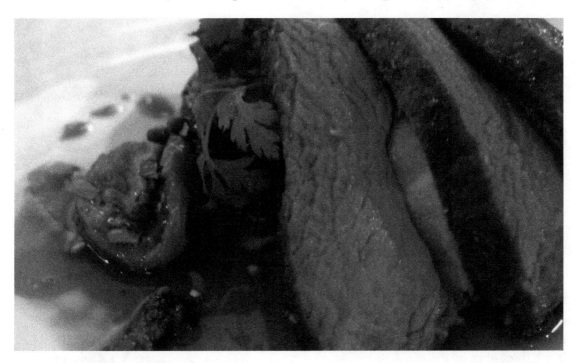

INGREDIENTS:

- 1 tsp. smoked paprika
- 1 tsp. cayenne pepper
- 1 tsp. onion powder
- 1 tsp. garlic powder
- Salt and freshly ground black pepper, to taste
- 3 lb. beef rump roast
- ¼ C. Worcestershire sauce

INSTRUCTIONS:

1. Set the temperature of Traeger Grill to 200 degrees F and preheat with closed lid for 15 mins, using charcoal.
2. In a bowl, mix together all spices.
3. Coat the rump roast with Worcestershire sauce evenly and then, rub with spice mixture generously.
4. Place the rump roast onto the grill and cook for about 5-6 hours.
5. Remove the roast from grill and place onto a cutting board for about 10-15 mins before serving.
6. With a sharp knife, cut the roast into desired-sized slices and serve.

NUTRITION INFORMATION:

Calories per serving: 252; Carbohydrates: 2.3g; Protein: 37.8g; Fat: 9.1g; Sugar: 1.8g; Sodium: 200mg; Fiber: 0.2g

STUNNING PRIME RIB ROAST

Serves: 10 | **Cooking Time:** 3 hours 50 mins | **Prep Time:** 10 mins

INGREDIENTS:

- 1 (5-lb.) prime rib roast
- Salt, to taste
- 5 tbsp. olive oil
- 4 tsp. dried rosemary, crushed
- 2 tsp. garlic powder
- 1 tsp. onion powder
- 1 tsp. paprika
- ½ tsp. cayenne pepper
- Freshly ground black pepper, to taste

INSTRUCTIONS:

1. Season the roast with salt generously.
2. With a plastic wrap, cover the roast and refrigerate for about 24 hours.
3. In a bowl, mix together remaining ingredients and set aside for about 1 hour.
4. Rub the roast with oil mixture from both sides evenly.
5. Arrange the roast in a large baking sheet and refrigerate for about 6-12 hours.
6. Set the temperature of Traeger Grill to 225-230 degrees F and preheat with closed lid for 15 mins. , using pecan wood chips.
7. Place the roast onto the grill and cook for about 3-3½ hours.
8. Meanwhile, preheat the oven to 500 degrees F.
9. Remove the roast from grill and place onto a large baking sheet.
10. Place the baking sheet in oven and roast for about 15-20 mins.
11. Remove the roast from oven and place onto a cutting board for about 10-15 mins before serving.
12. With a sharp knife, cut the roast into desired-sized slices and serve.

NUTRITION INFORMATION:

Calories per serving: 605; Carbohydrates: 3.8g; Protein: 38g; Fat: 47.6g; Sugar: 0.3g; Sodium: 1285mg; Fiber: 0.3g

REAL TREAT CHUCK ROAST

Serves: 8 | **Cooking Time:** 4½ hours | **Prep Time:** 10 mins

INGREDIENTS:

- 2 tbsp. onion powder
- 2 tbsp. garlic powder
- 1 tbsp. red chili powder
- 1 tbsp. cayenne pepper
- Salt and freshly ground black pepper, to taste
- 1 (3 lb.) beef chuck roast
- 16 fluid oz. warm beef broth

INSTRUCTIONS:

1. Set the temperature of Traeger Grill to 250 degrees F and preheat with closed lid for 15 mins.
2. In a bowl, mix together spices, salt and black pepper.
3. Rub the chuck roast with spice mixture evenly.
4. Place the rump roast onto the grill and cook for about 1½ hours per side.
5. Now, arrange chuck roast in a steaming pan with beef broth.
6. With a piece of foil, cover the pan and cook for about 2-3 hours.
7. Remove the chuck roast from grill and place onto a cutting board for about 20 mins before slicing.
8. With a sharp knife, cut the chuck roast into desired-sized slices and serve.

NUTRITION INFORMATION:

Calories per serving: 645; Carbohydrates: 4.2g; Protein: 46.4g; Fat: 48g; Sugar: 1.4g; Sodium: 329mg; Fiber: 1g

SIMPLY DELICIOUS TRI TIP ROAST

Serves: 8 | **Cooking Time:** 35 mins | **Prep Time:** 10 mins

INGREDIENTS:

- 1 tbsp. granulated onion
- 1 tbsp. granulated garlic
- Salt and freshly ground black pepper, to taste
- 1 (3-lb.) tri tip roast, trimmed

INSTRUCTIONS:

1. In a bowl, add all ingredients except for roast and mix well.
2. Coat the roast with spice mixture generously.
3. Set aside at room temperature until grill heats.
4. Set the temperature of Traeger Grill to 250 degrees F and preheat with closed lid for 15 mins.
5. Place the roast onto the grill and cook for about 25 mins.
6. Now, set the grill to 350-400 degrees F and preheat with closed lid for 15 mins. and sear roast for about 3-5 mins per side.
7. Remove the roast from grill and place onto a cutting board for about 15-20 mins before slicing.
8. With a sharp knife, cut the roast into slices across the grain and serve.

NUTRITION INFORMATION:

Calories per serving: 313; Carbohydrates:
0.8g; Protein: 45.7g; Fat: 14.2g; Sugar: 0.3g;
Sodium: 115mg; Fiber: 0.1g

INEXPENSIVE FLANK STEAK

Serves: 6 | **Cooking Time:** 30 mins | **Prep Time:** 15 mins

INGREDIENTS:

- 1 (2-lb.) beef flank steak
- 2 tbsp. olive oil
- ¼ C. BBQ rub
- 2 tbsp. butter, melted

INSTRUCTIONS:

1. Set the temperature of Traeger Grill to 225 degrees F and preheat with closed lid for 15 mins.
2. Coat the steak with oil evenly and season with BBQ rub.
3. Place the steak onto the grill and cook for about 10-15 mins per side.
4. Remove the steak from grill and place onto a cutting board for about 10 mins before slicing.
5. With a sharp knife, cut the steak into slices across the grain.
6. Drizzle with melted butter and serve.

NUTRITION INFORMATION:

Calories per serving: 355; Carbohydrates: 0g; Protein: 45.9g; Fat: 17.9g; Sugar: 0g; Sodium: 1607mg; Fiber: 0g

TENDER FLANK STEAK

Serves: 6 | **Cooking Time:** 10 mins | **Prep Time:** 15 mins

INGREDIENTS:

- ½ C. olive oil
- 1/3 C. fresh lemon juice
- 1/3 C. soy sauce
- ¼ C. brown sugar
- 2 tbsp. Worcestershire sauce
- 5 garlic cloves, minced
- 1 tsp. red chili powder
- 1 tsp. red pepper flakes, crushed
- 2 lb. flank steak

INSTRUCTIONS:

1. In a resealable plastic bag, add all ingredients except for steak and mix well.
2. Place the steak and seal the bag.
3. Shake the bag vigorously to coat well.
4. Refrigerate to marinate overnight.
5. Set the temperature of Traeger Grill to 450 degrees F and preheat with closed lid for 15 mins.
6. Place the steak onto the grill and cook for about 5 mins per side.
7. Remove the steak from grill and place onto a cutting board for about 10 mins before slicing.
8. With a sharp knife, cut the steak into slices across the grain.

NUTRITION INFORMATION:

Calories per serving: 482; Carbohydrates: 9.5g; Protein: 43.3g; Fat: 29.6g; Sugar: 7.5g; Sodium: 948mg; Fiber: 0.4g

RESTAURANT-STYLE RIB-EYE STEAK

Serves: 2 | **Cooking Time:** 20 mins | **Prep Time:** 10 mins

INGREDIENTS:

- 2 (1 3/8-inch thick) rib-eye steaks, trimmed
- 1 tbsp. olive oil
- 1 tbsp. steak seasoning

INSTRUCTIONS:

1. Coat both sides of each steak with oil and season with steak seasoning.
2. Set aside at room temperature for about 15 mins.
3. Set the temperature of Traeger Grill to 325 degrees F and preheat with closed lid for 15 mins.
4. Place the steaks onto the grill and cook for about 15-20 mins, flipping after every 6 mins.
5. Remove from grill and serve immediately.

NUTRITION INFORMATION:

Calories per serving: 527; Carbohydrates: 0g; Protein: 30.1g; Fat: 44.6; Sugar: 0g; Sodium: 98mg; Fiber: 0g

2-INGREDIENTS FILET MIGNON

Serves: 2 | **Cooking Time:** 10 mins | **Prep Time:** 10 mins

INGREDIENTS:

- 2 filet mignons
- Salt and freshly ground black pepper, to taste

INSTRUCTIONS:

1. Set the temperature of Traeger Grill to 450 degrees F and preheat with closed lid for 15 mins.
2. Season the steaks with salt and black pepper generously.
3. Place the filet mignons onto the grill and grill and cook for about 5 mins per side.
4. Remove from grill and serve immediately.

NUTRITION INFORMATION:

Calories per serving: 254; Carbohydrates: 0g; Protein: 39.8g; Fat: 9.3g; Sugar: 0g; Sodium: 161mg; Fiber: 0g

FALL-OF-THE-BONES SHORT RIBS

Serves: 4 | **Cooking Time:** 5½ hours | **Prep Time:** 15 mins

INGREDIENTS:

- 2½ lb. beef short ribs, trimmed
- 4 tbsp. extra-virgin olive oil
- 4 tbsp. beef rub
- 1 C. apple juice
- 1 C. apple cider vinegar
- 1 C. red wine
- 1 C. beef broth
- 2 tbsp. butter
- 2 tbsp. Worcestershire sauce
- Salt and freshly ground black pepper, to taste

INSTRUCTIONS:

1. Set the temperature of Traeger Grill to 225 degrees F and preheat with closed lid for 15 mins.
2. Coat the ribs with olive oil and season with rub evenly.
3. Arrange the ribs onto the grill and cook for about 1 hour.
4. In a food-safe spray bottle, mix together apple juice and vinegar.
5. After 1 hour spray the ribs with vinegar mixture evenly.
6. Cook for about 2 hours, spraying with vinegar mixture after every 15 mins.
7. In a bowl, mix together remaining ingredients.
8. Transfer the ribs in a baking dish with wine mixture.
9. With a piece of foil, cover the baking dish tightly and cook for about 2-2½ hours.
10. Remove the ribs from grill and place onto a cutting board for about 10-15 mins before slicing.
11. With a sharp knife, cut the ribs into equal-sized individual ribs and serve.

NUTRITION INFORMATION:

Calories per serving: 859; Carbohydrates: 10.9g; Protein: 83.2g; Fat: 45.7g; Sugar: 8.4g; Sodium: 532mg; Fiber: 0.1g

FAVORITE AMERICAN SHORT RIBS

Serves: 6 | **Cooking Time:** 3 hours | **Prep Time:** 15 mins

INGREDIENTS:

For Mustard Sauce:
- 1 C. prepared yellow mustard
- ¼ C. red wine vinegar
- ¼ C. dill pickle juice
- 2 tbsp. soy sauce
- 2 tbsp. Worcestershire sauce
- 1 tsp. ground ginger
- 1 tsp. granulated garlic

For Spice Rub:
- 2 tbsp. salt
- 2 tbsp. freshly ground black pepper
- 1 tbsp. white cane sugar
- 1 tbsp. granulated garlic

For Ribs:
- 6 (14-oz.) (4-5-inch long) beef short ribs

INSTRUCTIONS:

1. Set the temperature of Traeger Grill to 230-250 degrees F and preheat with closed lid for 15 mins, using charcoal.
2. For sauce: in a bowl, add all the ingredients and with a wire whisk, bet until well combined.
3. For rub: in a small bowl, mix together all ingredients.
4. Coat the ribs with sauce generously and then sprinkle with spice rub evenly.
5. Place the ribs onto the grill over indirect heat, bone side down and cook for about 1-1½ hours.
6. Flip the side and cook for about 45 mins.
7. Flip the side and cook for about 45 mins more.
8. Remove the ribs from grill and place onto a cutting board for about 10 mins before serving.

9. With a sharp knife, cut the ribs into equal-sized individual pieces and serve.

NUTRITION INFORMATION:

Calories per serving: 867; Carbohydrates: 7.7g; Protein: 117.1g; Fat: 37.5g; Sugar: 3.6g; Sodium: 3400mg; Fiber: 2.1g

SUPER-EASY SHORT RIBS

Serves: 8 | **Cooking Time:** 10 hours | **Prep Time:** 15 mins

INGREDIENTS:

- 2 tsp. smoked paprika
- 2 tsp. garlic powder
- Salt and freshly ground black pepper, to taste
- 1 (4-lb.) rack of beef short ribs, trimmed and silver skin removed
- 2 tbsp. olive oil
- 1 C. apple cider vinegar

INSTRUCTIONS:

1. Set the temperature of Traeger Grill to 250-250 degrees F and preheat with closed lid for 15 mins, using charcoal.
2. In a small bowl, mix together spices, salt and black pepper.
3. Coat ribs with oil evenly and then rub with spice mixture.
4. Place the ribs onto the grill over indirect heat, bone side down and cook for about 6-10 hours.
5. In a food-safe spray bottle, add apple cider vinegar.
6. After 5 hours, spray the ribs with vinegar evenly.
7. Remove the ribs from grill and place onto a cutting board for about 10 mins before serving.
8. With a sharp knife, cut the ribs into equal-sized individual pieces and serve.

NUTRITION INFORMATION:

Calories per serving: 461; Carbohydrates: 1.1g; Protein: 69g; Fat: 17.7g; Sugar: 0.3g; Sodium: 171mg; Fiber: 0.3g

TEXAS-STYLE BEEF RIBS

Serves: 4 | **Cooking Time:** 6 hours 3 mins | **Prep Time:** 15 mins

INGREDIENTS:

- 2 tbsp. butter
- 1 C. white vinegar
- 1 C. yellow mustard
- 2 tbsp. brown sugar
- 2 tbsp. Tabasco sauce
- 1 tsp. Worcestershire sauce
- 2 racks of beef ribs
- Salt and freshly ground black pepper, to taste

INSTRUCTIONS:

1. For BBQ sauce: in a pan, melt butter over medium heat. Stir in vinegar, mustard, brown sugar, Tabasco and Worcestershire sauce and remove from heat.
2. Set aside to cool completely.
3. Set the temperature of Traeger Grill to 225 degrees F and preheat with closed lid for 15 mins.
4. Season the rib racks with salt and black pepper evenly.
5. Coat rib rack with cooled sauce evenly.
6. Arrange the rib racks onto the grill and cook for about 5-6 hours, coating with sauce after every 2 hours.
7. Remove the rib racks from grill and place onto a cutting board for about 10-15 mins before slicing.
8. With a sharp knife, cut the rib racks into equal-sized individual ribs and serve.

NUTRITION INFORMATION:

Calories per serving: 504; Carbohydrates: 5.7g; Protein: 70.7g; Fat: 19.7g; Sugar: 3.6g; Sodium: 719mg; Fiber: 1.4g

DRUNKEN BEEF JERKY

Serves: 6 | **Cooking Time:** 5 hours | **Prep Time:** 15 mins

INGREDIENTS:

- 1 (12-oz.) bottle dark beer
- 1 C. soy sauce
- ¼ C. Worcestershire sauce
- 2 tbsp. hot sauce
- 3 tbsp. brown sugar
- 2 tbsp. coarse ground black pepper, divided
- 1 tbsp. curing salt
- ½ tsp. garlic salt
- 2 lb. flank steak, trimmed and cut into ¼-inch thick slices

INSTRUCTIONS:

1. In a bowl, add the beer, soy sauce, Worcestershire sauce, brown sugar, 2 tbsp. of black pepper, curing salt and garlic salt and mix well.
2. In a large resealable plastic bag, place the steak slices and marinade mixture.
3. Seal the bag, squeezing out the air and then shake to coat well.
4. Refrigerate to marinate overnight.
5. Set the temperature of Traeger Grill to 180 degrees F and preheat with closed lid for 15 mins.
6. Remove the steak slices from the bag and discard the marinade.
7. With paper towels, pat dry the steak slices.
8. Sprinkle the steak slices with remaining black pepper generously.
9. Arrange the steak slices onto the grill in a single layer and cook for about 4-5 hours.

NUTRITION INFORMATION:

Calories per serving: 374; Carbohydrates: 13.3g; Protein: 45.3g; Fat: 12.7g; Sugar: 7.2g; Sodium: 2700mg; Fiber: 0.9g

TERIYAKI BEEF JERKY

Serves: 9 | **Cooking Time:** 5 hours | **Prep Time:** 15 mins

INGREDIENTS:

- 3 lb. sirloin steaks, cut into ¼-inch thick slices
- 2 C. soy sauce
- ½ C. brown sugar
- 1 C. pineapple juice
- 2 tbsp. rice wine vinegar
- 2 tbsp. hoisin sauce
- 2 tbsp. Sriracha
- 2 tbsp. garlic, minced
- 2 tbsp. red pepper flakes, crushed
- 2 tsp. onion powder

INSTRUCTIONS:

1. In a large zip lock bag, place all ingredients.
2. Seal the bag, squeezing out the air and then shake to coat well.
3. Refrigerate to marinate for 6-24 hours.
4. Remove the bag from the refrigerator and set aside at room temperature for about 1 hour before cooking.
5. Set the temperature of Traeger Grill to 180-190 degrees F and preheat with closed lid for 15 mins.
6. Remove the steak slices from the bag and discard the marinade.
7. With paper towels, pat dry the steak slices.
8. Arrange the steak slices onto the grill in a single layer and cook for about 4-5 hours, flipping once after 2-2½ hours.

NUTRITION INFORMATION:

Calories per serving: 378; Carbohydrates: 19.8g; Protein: 50g; Fat: 9.8g; Sugar: 12.9g; Sodium: 3379mg; Fiber: 1g

COMFORTING BEEF MEATLOAF

Serves: 8 | **Cooking Time:** 2½ hours | **Prep Time:** 20 mins

INGREDIENTS:

For Meatloaf:
- 3 lb. ground beef
- 3 eggs
- ½ C. panko breadcrumbs
- 1 (10-oz.) can diced tomatoes with green chile peppers
- 1 large white onion, chopped
- 2 hot banana peppers, chopped
- 2 tbsp. seasoned salt
- 2 tsp. liquid smoke flavoring
- 2 tsp. smoked paprika
- 1 tsp. onion salt
- 1 tsp. garlic salt
- Salt and freshly ground black pepper, to taste

For Sauce:
- ½ C. ketchup
- ¼ C. tomato-based chile sauce
- ¼ C. white sugar
- 2 tsp. Worcestershire sauce
- 2 tsp. hot pepper sauce
- 1 tsp. red pepper flakes, crushed
- 1 tsp. red chili pepper
- Salt and freshly ground black pepper, to taste

INSTRUCTIONS:

1. Set the temperature of Traeger Grill to 225 degrees F and preheat with closed lid for 15 mins, using charcoal.
2. Grease a loaf pan.
3. For meatloaf: in a bowl, add all ingredients and with your hands, mix until well combined.
4. Place the mixture into prepared loaf pan evenly.
5. Place the pan onto the grill and cook for about 2 hours.
6. For sauce: in a bowl, add all ingredients and beat until well combined.
7. Remove the pan from grill and drain excess grease from meatloaf.
8. Place sauce over meatloaf evenly and place the pan onto the grill.
9. Cook for about 30 mins.
10. Remove the meatloaf from grill and set aside for about 10 mins before serving.
11. Carefully, invert the meatloaf onto a platter.
12. Cut the meatloaf into desired-sized slices and serve.

NUTRITION INFORMATION:

Calories per serving: 423; Carbohydrates: 15.7g; Protein: 54.9; Fat: 13; Sugar: 12.3g; Sodium: 299mg; Fiber: 1.5g

GLORIOUS PORK BACK RIBS

Serves: 16 | **Cooking Time:** 5 hours | **Prep Time:** 15 mins

INGREDIENTS:

- ¼ C. yellow honey mustard
- ¼ C. brown sugar
- 1/3 C. paprika
- ¼ C. garlic powder
- ¼ C. onion powder
- 2 tbsp. chipotle chili pepper flakes
- 1 tbsp. ground cumin
- Salt and freshly ground black pepper, to taste
- 2 tbsp. dried parsley flakes
- 8 lb. pork baby back ribs, silver skin removed

INSTRUCTIONS:

1. In a bowl, add all ingredients except for ribs and mix well.
2. Rub the pork ribs with spice mixture generously.
3. Set the temperature of Traeger Grill to 200 degrees F and preheat with closed lid for 15 mins, using charcoal.
4. Arrange the ribs onto the grill and cook for about 2 hours.
5. Remove the ribs from grill and wrap in heavy duty foil.
6. Cook for about 2 hours.
7. Remove the foil and cook for about 1 hour more.
8. Remove the ribs from grill and place onto a cutting board for about 10-15 mins before serving.

NUTRITION INFORMATION:

Calories per serving: 659; Carbohydrates: 7.8g; Protein: 61.1g; Fat: 40.7g; Sugar: 4.4g; Sodium: 186mg; Fiber: 1.5g

BBQ PARTY PORK RIBS

Serves: 6 | **Cooking Time:** 1 hour 55 mins | **Prep Time:** 20 mins

INGREDIENTS:

- 2 bone-in racks of pork ribs, silver skin removed
- 6 oz. BBQ rub
- 8 oz. apple juice
- ½ C. BBQ sauce

INSTRUCTIONS:

1. Coat each rack of ribs with BBQ rub generously.
2. Arrange the racks onto a platter and set aside for about 30 mins.
3. Set the temperature of Traeger Grill to 225 degrees F and preheat with closed lid for 15 mins.
4. Arrange the racks onto the grill, bone side down and cook for about 1 hour.
5. In a food-safe spray bottle, place apple juice.
6. Spray the racks with vinegar mixture evenly.
7. Cook for about 3½ hours, spraying with vinegar mixture after every 45 mins.
8. Now, coat the racks with a thin layer of BBQ sauce evenly and cook for about 10 mins more.
9. Remove the racks from grill and place onto a cutting board for about 10-15 mins before slicing.
10. With a sharp knife, cut each rack into individual ribs and serve.

NUTRITION INFORMATION:

Calories per serving: 801; Carbohydrates: 44.9g; Protein: 60.4g; Fat: 406g; Sugar: 37.4g; Sodium: 558mg; Fiber: 0.8g

SUMMERTIME PORK CHOPS

Serves: 4 | **Cooking Time:** 1 hour 35 mins | **Prep Time:** 15 mins

INGREDIENTS:

For Brine:
- 8 C. apple juice
- 1 C. light brown sugar
- ½ C. kosher salt
- ½ C. BBQ rub

For Pork Chops:
- 4 thick-cut pork loin chops
- 2 tbsp. BBQ rub
- 1 tbsp. Montreal steak seasoning

INSTRUCTIONS:

1. For brine: in a large pan, add 4 C. of apple juice and cook until heated completely.
2. Add sugar, salt and dry rub and cook until dissolved, stirring continuously.
3. Remove the pan from heat and stir in remaining apple juice.
4. Set aside to cool completely.
5. In a larger zip lock, add brine mixture and chops.
6. Seal the bag and refrigerate for about 2 hours.
7. Set the temperature of Traeger Grill to 250 degrees F and preheat with closed lid for 15 mins.
8. Remove the chops from brine and set aside for about 10-15 mins.
9. Now, season the chops with BBQ rub and steak seasoning evenly
10. Place the chops onto the grill and cook for about 1½ hours.
11. Remove the chops from grill and set aside for about 5 mins before serving.

NUTRITION INFORMATION:

Calories per serving: 609; Carbohydrates: 92.6g; Protein: 29.5; Fat: 12.6; Sugar: 84.2g; Sodium: 299mg; Fiber: 1g

MIDWEEK DINNER PORK TENDERLOIN

Serves: 6　|　**Cooking Time:** 3 hours　|　**Prep Time:** 10 mins

INGREDIENTS:

- ½ C. apple cider
- 3 tbsp. honey
- 2 (1¼-1½-lb.) pork tenderloins, silver skin removed
- 3 tbsp. sweet rub

INSTRUCTIONS:

1. In a small bowl, mix together apple cider and honey.
2. Coat the outside of tenderloins with honey mixture and season with the rub generously.
3. With a plastic wrap, cover each tenderloin and refrigerate for about 2-3 hours.
4. Set the temperature of Traeger Grill to 225 degrees F and preheat with closed lid for 15 mins.
5. Arrange the tenderloins onto the grill and cook for about 2½-3 hours.
6. Remove the pork tenderloins from grill and place onto a cutting board for about 10 mins before slicing.
7. With a sharp knife, cut each pork tenderloin into desired-sized slices and serve.

NUTRITION INFORMATION:

Calories per serving: 498; Carbohydrates: 11.1g; Protein: 67.8g; Fat: 18.4g; Sugar: 10.9g; Sodium: 146mg; Fiber: 0g

FLAVORSOME PORK LOIN

Serves: 8 | **Cooking Time:** 1 hour 40 mins | **Prep Time:** 15 mins

INGREDIENTS:

- 1 (12-oz.) bottle German lager
- 1/3 C. honey
- 2 tbsp. Dijon mustard
- 1 tsp. dried thyme
- 1 tsp. caraway seeds
- 1 (3-lb.) pork loin, silver skin removed
- 1 large Vidalia onion, chopped
- 3 garlic cloves, minced
- 3 tbsp. dry seasoned pork rub

INSTRUCTIONS:

1. In a bowl, add German lager, honey, Dijon mustard, thyme and caraway seeds and mix well.
2. In a large sealable Ziploc bag, place pork loin, onion, garlic and honey mixture.
3. Seal the bag and shake to coat well.
4. Refrigerate to marinate overnight.
5. Set the temperature of Traeger Grill to 350 degrees F and preheat with closed lid for 15 mins.
6. Remove the pork loin, onions and garlic from bag and place onto a plate.
7. Rub the pork loin with pork rub evenly.
8. Place the seasoned pork, onions, and garlic into a large roasting pan.
9. Arrange the pork tenderloin, fat side pointed up.
10. Place the marinade into a pan over medium heat and to a boil.
11. Cook for about 3-5 mins or until the liquid reduces by half.
12. Remove from the heat and set aside.
13. Place the roasting pan onto the grill and cook for about 1 hour.
14. Carefully pour the reduced marinade on top of the pork loin evenly.
15. Cook for another 30-60 mins, basting the meat with marinade occasionally.
16. Remove from the grill and place the pork loin onto a cutting board for about 10 mins before slicing.
17. With a sharp knife, cut each pork tenderloin into desired-sized slices and serve with the topping of pan juices.

NUTRITION INFORMATION:

Calories per serving: 492; Carbohydrates: 16.3g; Protein: 47.2g; Fat: 23.9g; Sugar: 12.8g; Sodium: 277mg; Fiber: 0.6g

BEST PORK BUTT ROAST

Serves: 14 | **Cooking Time:** 14 hours | **Prep Time:** 10 mins

INGREDIENTS:

- ¼ C. brown sugar
- 2 tbsp. New Mexico chile powder
- 2 tbsp. garlic powder
- Salt, to taste
- 1 (7-lb.) fresh pork butt roast

INSTRUCTIONS:

1. Set the temperature of Traeger Grill to 200-225 degrees F and preheat with closed lid for 15 mins.
2. In a bowl, place all ingredients except for pork roast and mix well.
3. Rub the pork roast with spice mixture generously.
4. Arrange a roasting rack in a drip pan.
5. Place the pork roast onto the rack in drip pan.
6. Place the drip pan onto the grill and cook for about 8-14 hours or until desired doneness.
7. Remove the roast from grill and place onto a cutting board for about 10-15 mins before slicing.
8. With a sharp knife, cut the roast into desired-sized slices and serve.

NUTRITION INFORMATION:

Calories per serving: 439; Carbohydrates: 4g; Protein: 40.g; Fat: 28.3g; Sugar: 2.9g; Sodium: 164mg; Fiber: 0.5g

FAJITA FAVORITE PORK SHOULDER

Serves: 20 | **Cooking Time:** 10 hours | **Prep Time:** 15 mins

INGREDIENTS:

For Brine:
- 4 C. hot water
- 1 C. kosher salt
- ¼ C. brown sugar
- 2 tbsp. black peppercorn
- 12 C. cold water
- 8 C. apple cider
- ¼ C. apple cider vinegar
- ¼ C. Worcestershire sauce

For Pork:
- 8½ pounds pork shoulder roast, trimmed
- ¼-½ C. pork rub

INSTRUCTIONS:

1. For brine: in a large container, add the hot water, salt, brown sugar and peppercorn and stir until completely dissolved.
2. Add the cold water, apple cider, vinegar and Worcestershire sauce and mix until well combined.
3. With a sharp knife, score the pork on both sides and place in the brine.
4. Cover the container and refrigerate for 24 hours.
5. Remove the pork from container and discard the brine.
6. Rinse the pork shoulder under running cold water thoroughly.
7. With paper towels, pat dry the pork shoulder completely.
8. Rub the pork shoulder with pork rub generously.
9. Place the pork shoulder onto a baking sheet and refrigerate for 2 hours or up to overnight.
10. Set the temperature of Traeger Grill to 150-160 degrees F and preheat with closed lid for 15 mins.
11. Place the pork shoulder onto the grill and cook for about 4 hours.
12. Now, set the temperature of Traeger Grill to 250 degrees F and cook for about 4-6 hours.
13. Remove the pork shoulder from grill and place onto a baking sheet for about 40-60 mins.
14. With two forks, shred the meat and serve.

NUTRITION INFORMATION:

40

Calories per serving: 626; Carbohydrates: 15g; Protein: 45g; Fat: 41.4g; Sugar: 13.5g; Sodium: 5890mg; Fiber: 0.3g

SIMPLEST PORK BELLY

Serves: 12 | **Cooking Time:** 8 hours | **Prep Time:** 10 mins

INGREDIENTS:

- 1 (5-lb.) pork belly, skin removed
- Kosher salt and coarsely ground black pepper, to taste

INSTRUCTIONS:

1. Set the temperature of Traeger Grill to 225 degrees F and preheat with closed lid for 15 mins, using charcoal.
2. Rub the pork belly with salt and black pepper generously.
3. Arrange the pork belly onto the grill and cook for about 6-8 hours,
4. Remove the pork belly from grill and place onto a cutting board for about 10-15 mins before slicing.
5. With a sharp knife, cut the pork belly into desired-sized slices and serve.

NUTRITION INFORMATION:

Calories per serving: 534; Carbohydrates: 0g; Protein: 28.9g; Fat: 46.7g; Sugar: 0g; Sodium: 790mg; Fiber: 0g

BEAUTIFUL CHRISTMAS HAM

Serves: 16 | **Cooking Time:** 1 hour 20 mins | **Prep Time:** 15 mins

INGREDIENTS:

- 1 C. honey
- ¼ C. dark corn syrup
- 1 (7-lb.) ready-to-eat ham
- ¼ C. whole cloves
- ½ C. butter, softened

INSTRUCTIONS:

1. Set the temperature of Traeger Grill to 325 degrees F and preheat with closed lid for 15 mins, using charcoal.
2. In a small pan, add honey and corn syrup and cook until heated slightly, stirring continuously.
3. Remove the pan of glaze from heat and set aside.
4. With a sharp knife, score the ham in a cross pattern.
5. Insert whole cloves at the crossings.
6. Coat the ham with butter evenly.
7. Arrange ham in foil-lined roasting pan and top with ¾ of glaze evenly.
8. Place the pan onto the grill and cook for about 1¼ hours, coating with remain glaze after every 10-15 mins.
9. Remove the ham from grill and place onto a cutting board for about 20-25 mins before serving.
10. With a sharp knife, cut the ham into desired-sized slices and serve.

NUTRITION INFORMATION:

Calories per serving: 457; Carbohydrates: 29.7g; Protein: 33.2g; Fat: 23.1g; Sugar: 18.7g; Sodium: 2633mg; Fiber: 3.2g

BACKYARD COOKOUT SAUSAGES

Serves: 6 | **Cooking Time:** 23 mins | **Prep Time:** 15 mins

INGREDIENTS:

- ½ C. apricot jam
- 1 tbsp. Dijon mustard
- 12 breakfast sausage links

INSTRUCTIONS:

1. Set the temperature of Traeger Grill to 350 degrees F and preheat with closed lid for 15 mins.
2. In a small pan, add jam and mustard over medium-low heat and cook until warmed.
3. Reduce the heat to low to keep the glaze warm.
4. Arrange the sausage links onto grill and cook for about 10-15 mins, flipping twice.
5. Coat the sausage links with jam glaze evenly and cook for about 2-3 mins.
6. Remove the sausage links from grill and serve alongside the remaining glaze.

NUTRITION INFORMATION:

Calories per serving: 575; Carbohydrates: 17.3g; Protein: 29.5g; Fat: 42.7g; Sugar: 11.6g; Sodium: 1164mg; Fiber: 0.2g

ELEGANT LAMB CHOPS

Serves: 4 | **Cooking Time:** 30 mins | **Prep Time:** 15 mins

INGREDIENTS:

- 4 lamb shoulder chops
- 4 C. buttermilk
- 1 C. cold water
- ¼ C. kosher salt
- 2 tbsp. olive oil
- 1 tbsp. Texas-style rub

INSTRUCTIONS:

1. In a large bowl, add buttermilk, water and salt and stir until salt is dissolved.
2. Add chops and coat with mixture evenly.
3. Refrigerate for at least 4 hours.
4. Remove the chops from bowl and rinse under cold running water.
5. Coat the chops with olive oil and then sprinkle with rub evenly.
6. Set the temperature of Traeger Grill to 240 degrees F and preheat with closed lid for 15 mins, using charcoal.
7. Arrange the chops onto grill and cook for about 25-30 mins or until desired doneness.
8. Meanwhile, preheat the broiler of oven. Grease a broiler pan.

1. Remove the chops from grill and place onto the prepared broiler pan.
2. Transfer the broiler pan into the oven and broil for about 3-5 mins or until browned.
3. Remove the chops from oven and serve hot.

NUTRITION INFORMATION:

Calories per serving: 414; Carbohydrates: 11.7g; Protein: 5.6g; Fat: 22.7g; Sugar: 11.7g; Sodium: 7000mg; Fiber: 0g

EASY-TO-PREPARE LAMB CHOPS

Serves: 6 | **Cooking Time:** 12 mins | **Prep Time:** 10 mins

INGREDIENTS:

- 6 (6-oz.) lamb chops
- 3 tbsp. olive oil
- Salt and freshly ground black pepper, to taste

INSTRUCTIONS:

1. Set the temperature of Traeger Grill to 450 degrees F and preheat with closed lid for 15 mins.
2. Coat the lamb chops with oil and then, season with salt and black pepper evenly.
3. Arrange the chops onto the grill and cook for about 4-6 mins per side.
4. Remove the chops from grill and serve hot.

NUTRITION INFORMATION:

Calories per serving: 376; Carbohydrates: 0g; Protein: 47.8g; Fat: 19.5g; Sugar: 0g; Sodium: 156mg; Fiber: 0g

FOOLPROOF LAMB CHOPS

Serves: 4 | **Cooking Time:** 17 mins | **Prep Time:** 15 mins

INGREDIENTS:

- ½ C. extra-virgin olive oil, divided
- ¼ C. onion, chopped roughly
- 2 garlic cloves, chopped roughly
- 2 tbsp. balsamic vinegar
- 2 tbsp. soy sauce
- 1 tsp. Worcestershire sauce
- 1 tbsp. fresh rosemary, chopped
- 2 tsp. Dijon mustard
- Freshly ground black pepper, to taste
- 4 (5-oz.) lamb chops
- Salt, to taste

INSTRUCTIONS:

1. In a small pan, heat 1 tbsp. of olive oil over medium heat and sauté the onion and garlic for about 4-5 mins.
2. Remove from the heat and transfer into a blender.
3. In the blender, add the vinegar, soy sauce, Worcestershire sauce, rosemary, mustard and black pepper and pulse until well combined.
4. While the motor is running, slowly add the remaining oil and pulse until smooth.
5. Transfer the sauce into a bowl and set aside.
6. Set the temperature of Traeger Grill to 500 degrees F and preheat with closed lid for 15 mins.
7. Coat the lamb chops with remaining oil and then, season with salt and black pepper evenly.
8. Arrange the chops onto the grill and cook for about 4-6 mins per side.
9. Remove the chops from grill and serve hot alongside the sauce.

NUTRITION INFORMATION:

Calories per serving: 496; Carbohydrates: 2.8g; Protein: 40.6g; Fat: 35.8g; Sugar: 0.8g; Sodium: 641mg; Fiber: 0.7g

DELICIOUSLY SPICY RACK OF LAMB

Serves: 6 | **Cooking Time:** 3 hours | **Prep Time:** 15 mins

INGREDIENTS:

- 2 tbsp. paprika
- ½ tbsp. coriander seeds
- 1 tsp. cumin seeds
- 1 tsp. ground allspice
- 1 tsp. lemon peel powder
- Salt and freshly ground black pepper, to taste
- 2 (1½-lb.) rack of lamb ribs, trimmed

INSTRUCTIONS:

1. Set the temperature of Traeger Grill to 225 degrees F and preheat with closed lid for 15 mins.

2. In a coffee grinder, add all ingredients except rib racks and grind into a powder.

3. Coat the rib racks with spice mixture generously.

4. Arrange the rib racks onto the grill and cook for about 3 hours.

5. Remove the rib racks from grill and place onto a cutting board for about 10-15 mins before slicing.

6. With a sharp knife, cut the rib racks into equal-sized individual ribs and serve.

NUTRITION INFORMATION:

Calories per serving: 545; Carbohydrates: 1.7g; Protein: 64.4g; Fat: 29.7g; Sugar: 0.3g; Sodium: 221mg; Fiber: 1g

AROMATIC HERBED RACK OF LAMB

Serves: 3 | **Cooking Time:** 2 hours | **Prep Time:** 15 mins

INGREDIENTS:

- 2 tbsp. fresh sage
- 2 tbsp. fresh rosemary
- 2 tbsp. fresh thyme
- 2 garlic cloves, peeled
- 1 tbsp. honey
- Salt and freshly ground black pepper, to taste
- ¼ C. olive oil
- 1 (1½-lb.) rack of lamb, trimmed

INSTRUCTIONS:

1. In a food processor, add all ingredients except for oil and rack of lamb rack and pulse until well combined.
2. While motor is running, slowly add oil and pulse until a smooth paste is formed.
3. Coat the rib rack with paste generously and refrigerate for about 2 hours.
4. Set the temperature of Traeger Grill to 225 degrees F and preheat with closed lid for 15 mins.
5. Arrange the rack of lamb onto the grill and cook for about 2 hours.
6. Remove the rack of lamb from grill and place onto a cutting board for about 10-15 mins before slicing.
7. With a sharp knife, cut the rack into individual ribs and serve.

NUTRITION INFORMATION:

Calories per serving: 566; Carbohydrates: 9.8g; Protein: 46.7g; Fat: 33.5g; Sugar: 5.8g; Sodium: 214mg; Fiber: 2.2g

HOLIDAY DINNER LEG OF LAMB

Serves: 8 | **Cooking Time:** 5 hours | **Prep Time:** 15 mins

INGREDIENTS:

- ½ C. olive oil
- ½ C. red wine vinegar
- ½ C. dry white wine
- 1 tbsp. garlic, minced
- 1 tsp. dried marjoram, crushed
- 1 tsp. dried rosemary, crushed
- Salt and freshly ground black pepper, to taste
- 1 (5-lb.) leg of lamb

INSTRUCTIONS:

1. In a bowl, add all ingredients except for leg of lamb and mix until well combined.
2. In a large resealable bag, add marinade and leg of lamb.
3. Seal the bag and shake to coat completely.
4. Refrigerate for about 4-6 hours, flipping occasionally.
5. Set the temperature of Traeger Grill to 225 degrees F and preheat with closed lid for 15 mins.
6. Place the leg of lamb onto the grill and cook for about 4-5 hours.
7. Remove the leg of lamb from grill and place onto a cutting board for about 20 mins before slicing.
8. With a sharp knife, cut the leg of lamb into desired-sized slices and serve.

NUTRITION INFORMATION:

Calories per serving: 653; Carbohydrates: 1g; Protein: 79.7g; Fat: 33.4g; Sugar: 0.2g; Sodium: 237mg; Fiber: 0.1g

FANCY GATHERING'S LAMB SHOULDER

Serves: 8 | **Cooking Time:** 2½ hours | **Prep Time:** 15 mins

INGREDIENTS:

- 1 (5-lb.) bone-in lamb shoulder, trimmed
- 2 tbsp. olive oil
- 1 tbsp. fresh lemon juice
- 1 tbsp. fresh ginger, peeled
- 4-6 garlic cloves, peeled
- ½ tbsp. ground cumin
- ½ tbsp. paprika
- ½ tbsp. ground turmeric
- ½ tbsp. ground allspice
- Salt and freshly ground black pepper, to taste

INSTRUCTIONS:

1. With a sharp knife, score the skin of the lamb shoulder into a diamond pattern.
2. In a food processor, add remaining all ingredients and pulse until smooth.
3. Coat the lamb shoulder with pureed mixture generously.
4. Arrange the lamb shoulder into a large baking dish and refrigerate, covered overnight.
5. Remove the baking dish of shoulder from refrigerator and set aside at room temperature for at least 1 hour before cooking.
6. Set the temperature of Traeger Grill to 225 degrees F and preheat with closed lid for 15 mins.
7. Place the lamb shoulder onto the grill and cook for about 2½ hours.
8. Remove the lamb shoulder from grill and place onto a cutting board for about 20 mins before slicing.
9. With a sharp knife, cut the lamb shoulder into desired-sized slices and serve.

NUTRITION INFORMATION:

Calories per serving: 41; Carbohydrates: 2g; Protein: 58.1g; Fat: 18.8g; Sugar: 0.1g; Sodium: 222mg; Fiber: 0.5g

SPICY & TANGY LAMB SHOULDER

Serves: 6 | **Cooking Time:** 5¾ hours | **Prep Time:** 15 mins

INGREDIENTS:

- 1 (5-lb.) bone-in lamb shoulder, trimmed
- 3-4 tbsp. Moroccan seasoning
- 2 tbsp. olive oil
- 1 C. water
- ¼ C. apple cider vinegar

INSTRUCTIONS:

1. Set the temperature of Traeger Grill to 275 degrees F and preheat with closed lid for 15 mins, using charcoal.
2. Coat the lamb shoulder with oil evenly and then rub with Moroccan seasoning generously.
3. Place the lamb shoulder onto the grill and cook for about 45 mins.
4. In a food-safe spray bottle, mix together vinegar and water.
5. Spray the lamb shoulder with vinegar mixture evenly.
6. Cook for about 4-5 hours, spraying with vinegar mixture after every 20 mins.
7. Remove the lamb shoulder from grill and place onto a cutting board for about 20 mins before slicing.
8. With a sharp knife, cut the lamb shoulder in desired sized slices and serve.

NUTRITION INFORMATION:

Calories per serving: 563; Carbohydrates: 3.1g; Protein: 77.4g; Fat: 25.2g; Sugar: 1.4g; Sodium: 1192mg; Fiber: 0g

WINE BRAISED LAMB SHANK

Serves: 2 | **Cooking Time:** 10 hours | **Prep Time:** 15 mins

INGREDIENTS:

- 2 (1¼-lb.) lamb shanks
- 1-2 C. water
- ¼ C. brown sugar
- 1/3 C. rice wine
- 1/3 C. soy sauce
- 1 tbsp. dark sesame oil
- 4 (1½x½-inch) orange zest strips
- 2 (3-inch long) cinnamon sticks
- 1½ tsp. Chinese five-spice powder

INSTRUCTIONS:

1. Set the temperature of Traeger Grill to 225-250 degrees F and preheat with closed lid for 15 mins. , using charcoal and soaked apple wood chips.

2. With a sharp knife, pierce each lamb shank at many places.
3. In a bowl, add remaining all ingredients and mix until sugar is dissolved.
4. In a large foil pan, place the lamb shanks and top with sugar mixture evenly.
5. Place the foil pan onto the grill and cook for about 8-10 hours, flipping after every 30 mins. (If required, add enough water to keep the liquid ½-inch over).
6. Remove from the grill and serve hot.

NUTRITION INFORMATION:

Calories per serving: 1200; Carbohydrates: 39.7g; Protein: 161.9g; Fat: 48.4; Sugar: 29g; Sodium: 2000mg; Fiber: 0.3g

CHEESY LAMB BURGERS

Serves: 4 | **Cooking Time:** 20 mins | **Prep Time:** 15 mins

INGREDIENTS:

- 2 lb. ground lamb
- 1 C. Parmigiano-Reggiano cheese, grated
- Salt and freshly ground black pepper, to taste

INSTRUCTIONS:

1. Set the temperature of Traeger Grill to 425 degrees F and preheat with closed lid for 15 mins.
2. In a bowl, add all ingredients and mix well.
3. Make 4 (¾-inch thick) patties from mixture.
4. With your thumbs, make a shallow but wide depression in each patty.
5. Arrange the patties onto the grill, depression-side down and cook for about 8 mins.
6. Flip and cook for about 8-10 mins.
7. Serve immediately.

NUTRITION INFORMATION:

Calories per serving: 502; Carbohydrates: 0g; Protein: 71.7g; Fat: 22.6g; Sugar: 0g; Sodium: 331mg; Fiber: 0g

POULTRY RECIPES

SPECIAL OCCASION'S DINNER CORNISH HEN

Serves: 4 | **Cooking Time:** 1 hour | **Prep Time:** 15 mins

INGREDIENTS:

- 4 Cornish game hens
- 4 fresh rosemary sprigs
- 4 tbsp. butter, melted
- 4 tsp. chicken rub

INSTRUCTIONS:

1. Set the temperature of Traeger Grill to 375 degrees F and preheat with closed lid for 15 mins.
2. With paper towels, pat dry the hens.
3. Tuck the wings behind the backs and with kitchen strings, tie the legs together.
4. Coat the outside of each hen with melted butter and sprinkle with rub evenly.
5. Stuff the cavity of each hen with a rosemary sprig.
6. Place the hens onto the grill and cook for about 50-60 mins.
7. Remove the hens from grill and place onto a platter for about 10 mins.
8. Cut each hen into desired-sized pieces and serve.

NUTRITION INFORMATION:

Calories per serving: 430; Carbohydrates: 2.1g; Protein: 25.4g; Fat: 33g; Sugar: 0g; Sodium: 331mg; Fiber: 0.7g

CRISPY & JUICY CHICKEN

Serves: 6 | **Cooking Time:** 5 hours | **Prep Time:** 15 mins

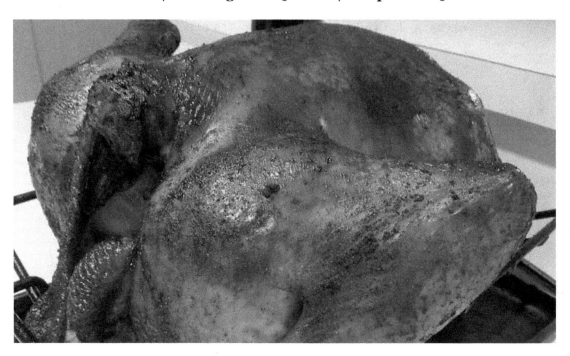

INGREDIENTS:

- ¾ C. dark brown sugar
- ½ C. ground espresso beans
- 1 tbsp. ground cumin
- 1 tbsp. ground cinnamon
- 1 tbsp. garlic powder
- 1 tbsp. cayenne pepper
- Salt and freshly ground black pepper, to taste
- 1 (4-lb.) whole chicken, neck and giblets removed

INSTRUCTIONS:

1. Set the temperature of Traeger Grill to 200-225 degrees F and preheat with closed lid for 15 mins.
2. In a bowl, mix together brown sugar, ground espresso, spices, salt and black pepper.
3. Rub the chicken with spice mixture generously.
4. Place the chicken onto the grill and cook for about 3-5 hours.
5. Remove chicken from grill and place onto a cutting board for about 10 mins before carving.
6. With a sharp knife, cut the chicken into desired-sized pieces and serve.

NUTRITION INFORMATION:

Calories per serving: 540; Carbohydrates: 20.7g; Protein: 88.3g; Fat: 9.6g; Sugar: 18.1g; Sodium: 226mg; Fiber: 1.2g

ULTIMATE TASTY CHICKEN

Serves: 5 | **Cooking Time:** 3 hours | **Prep Time:** 15 mins

INGREDIENTS:

For Brine:
- 1 C. brown sugar
- ½ C. kosher salt
- 16 C. water

For Chicken:
- 1 (3-lb.) whole chicken
- 1 tbsp. garlic, crushed
- 1 tsp. onion powder
- Salt and freshly ground black pepper, to taste
- 1 medium yellow onion, quartered
- 3 whole garlic cloves, peeled
- 1 lemon, quartered
- 4-5 fresh thyme sprigs

INSTRUCTIONS:

1. For brine: in a bucket, dissolve brown sugar and kosher salt in water.
2. Place the chicken in brine and refrigerate overnight.
3. Set the temperature of Traeger Grill to 225 degrees F and preheat with closed lid for 15 mins.
4. Remove the chicken from brine and with paper towels, pat it dry.
5. In a small bowl, mix together crushed garlic, onion powder, salt and black pepper.
6. Rub the chicken with garlic mixture evenly.
7. Stuff the cavity of chicken with onion, garlic cloves, lemon and thyme.
8. With kitchen strings, tie the legs together.
9. Place the chicken onto grill and cook, covered for about 2½-3 hours.
10. Remove chicken from pallet grill and transfer onto a cutting board for about 10 mins before carving.
11. With a sharp knife, cut the chicken in desired sized pieces and serve.

NUTRITION INFORMATION:

Calories per serving: 641; Carbohydrates: 31.7g; Protein: 79.2g; Fat: 20.2g; Sugar: 29.3g; Sodium: 11500mg; Fiber: 0.6g

SOUTH-EAST-ASIAN CHICKEN DRUMSTICKS

Serves: 6 | **Cooking Time:** 2 hours | **Prep Time:** 15 mins

INGREDIENTS:

- 1 C. fresh orange juice
- ¼ C. honey
- 2 tbsp. sweet chili sauce
- 2 tbsp. hoisin sauce
- 2 tbsp. fresh ginger, grated finely
- 2 tbsp. garlic, minced
- 1 tsp. Sriracha
- ½ tsp. sesame oil
- 6 chicken drumsticks

INSTRUCTIONS:

1. Set the temperature of Traeger Grill to 225 degrees F and preheat with closed lid for 15 mins, using charcoal.

2. In a bowl, place all ingredients except for chicken drumsticks and mix until well combined.

3. Reserve half of honey mixture in a small bowl.

4. In the bowl of remaining sauce, add drumsticks and mix well.

5. Arrange the chicken drumsticks onto the grill and cook for about 2 hours, basting with remaining sauce occasionally.

6. Serve hot.

NUTRITION INFORMATION:

Calories per serving: 385; Carbohydrates: 22.7g; Protein: 47.6g; Fat: 10.5g; Sugar: 18.6g; Sodium: 270mg; Fiber: 0.6g

GAME DAY CHICKEN DRUMSTICKS

Serves: 8 | **Cooking Time:** 1 hour | **Prep Time:** 15 mins

INGREDIENTS:

For Brine:
- ½ C. brown sugar
- ½ C. kosher salt
- 5 C. water
- 2 (12-oz.) bottles beer
- 8 chicken drumsticks

For Coating:
- ¼ C. olive oil
- ½ C. BBQ rub
- 1 tbsp. fresh parsley, minced
- 1 tbsp. fresh chives, minced
- ¾ C. BBQ sauce
- ¼ C. beer

INSTRUCTIONS:

1. For brine: in a bucket, dissolve brown sugar and kosher salt in water and beer.
2. Place the chicken drumsticks in brine and refrigerate, covered for about 3 hours.
3. Set the temperature of Traeger Grill to 275 degrees F and preheat with closed lid for 15 mins.
4. Remove chicken drumsticks from brine and rinse under cold running water.
5. With paper towels, pat dry chicken drumsticks.
6. Coat drumsticks with olive oil and rub with BBQ rub evenly.
7. Sprinkle the drumsticks with parsley and chives.
8. Arrange the chicken drumsticks onto the grill and cook for about 45 mins.
9. Meanwhile, in a bowl, mix together BBQ sauce and beer.
10. Remove from grill and coat the drumsticks with BBQ sauce evenly.
11. Cook for about 15 mins more.
12. Serve immediately.

NUTRITION INFORMATION:

Calories per serving: 448; Carbohydrates: 20.5g; Protein: 47.2g; Fat: 16.1g; Sugar: 14.9g; Sodium: 9700mg; Fiber: 0.2g

GLAZED CHICKEN THIGHS

Serves: 4 | **Cooking Time:** 30 mins | **Prep Time:** 15 mins

INGREDIENTS:

- 2 garlic cloves, minced
- ¼ C. honey
- 2 tbsp. soy sauce
- ¼ tsp. red pepper flakes, crushed
- 4 (5-oz.) skinless, boneless chicken thighs
- 2 tbsp. olive oil
- 2 tsp. sweet rub
- ¼ tsp. red chili powder
- Freshly ground black pepper, to taste

INSTRUCTIONS:

1. Set the temperature of Traeger Grill to 400 degrees F and preheat with closed lid for 15 mins.

2. In a small bowl, add garlic, honey, soy sauce and red pepper flakes and with a wire whisk, beat until well combined.

3. Coat chicken thighs with oil and season with sweet rub, chili powder and black pepper generously.

4. Arrange the chicken drumsticks onto the grill and cook for about 15 mins per side.

5. In the last 4-5 mins of cooking, coat the thighs with garlic mixture.

6. Serve immediately.

NUTRITION INFORMATION:

Calories per serving: 309; Carbohydrates: 18.7g; Protein: 32.3g; Fat: 12.1g; Sugar: 17.6g; Sodium: 504mg; Fiber: 0.2g

CAJUN CHICKEN BREASTS

Serves: 6 | **Cooking Time:** 6 hours | **Prep Time:** 10 mins

INGREDIENTS:

- 2 lb. skinless, boneless chicken breasts
- 2 tbsp. Cajun seasoning
- 1 C. BBQ sauce

INSTRUCTIONS:

1. Set the temperature of Traeger Grill to 225 degrees F and preheat with closed lid for 15 mins.
2. Rub the chicken breasts with Cajun seasoning generously.
3. Place the chicken breasts onto the grill and cook for about 4-6 hours.
4. During last hour of cooking, coat the breasts with BBQ sauce twice.
5. Serve hot.

NUTRITION INFORMATION:

Calories per serving: 252; Carbohydrates: 15.1g; Protein: 33.8g; Fat: 5.5g; Sugar: 10.9g; Sodium: 570mg; Fiber: 0.3g

BBQ SAUCE SMOTHERED CHICKEN BREASTS

Serves: 4 | **Cooking Time:** 30 mins | **Prep Time:** 15 mins

INGREDIENTS:

- 1 tsp. garlic, crushed
- ¼ C. olive oil
- 1 tbsp. Worcestershire sauce
- 1 tbsp. sweet mesquite seasoning
- 4 chicken breasts
- 2 tbsp. regular BBQ sauce
- 2 tbsp. spicy BBQ sauce
- 2 tbsp. honey bourbon BBQ sauce

INSTRUCTIONS:

1. Set the temperature of Traeger Grill to 450 degrees F and preheat with closed lid for 15 mins.

2. In a large bowl, mix together garlic, oil, Worcestershire sauce and mesquite seasoning.
3. Coat chicken breasts with seasoning mixture evenly.
4. Place the chicken breasts onto the grill and cook for about 20-30 mins.
5. Meanwhile, in a bowl, mix together all 3 BBQ sauces.
6. In the last 4-5 mins of cooking, coat breast with BBQ sauce mixture.
7. Serve hot.

NUTRITION INFORMATION:

Calories per serving: 421; Carbohydrates: 10.1g; Protein: 41,2g; Fat: 23.3g; Sugar: 6.9g; Sodium: 763mg; Fiber: 0.2g

BUDGET FRIENDLY CHICKEN LEGS

Serves: 6 | **Cooking Time:** 1½ hours | **Prep Time:** 15 mins

INGREDIENTS:

For Brine:
- 1 C. kosher salt
- ¾ C. light brown sugar
- 16 C. water
- 6 chicken leg quarters

For Glaze:
- ½ C. mayonnaise
- 2 tbsp. BBQ rub
- 2 tbsp. fresh chives, minced
- 1 tbsp. garlic, minced

INSTRUCTIONS:

1. For brine: in a bucket, dissolve salt and brown sugar in water.
2. Place the chicken quarters in brine and refrigerate, covered for about 4 hours.
3. Set the temperature of Traeger Grill to 275 degrees F and preheat with closed lid for 15 mins.
4. Remove chicken quarters from brine and rinse under cold running water.
5. With paper towels, pat dry chicken quarters.
6. For glaze: in a bowl, add all ingredients and mix till ell combined.
7. Coat chicken quarters with glaze evenly.
8. Place the chicken leg quarters onto grill and cook for about 1-1½ hours.
9. Serve immediately.

NUTRITION INFORMATION:

Calories per serving: 399; Carbohydrates: 17.2g; Protein: 29.1g; Fat: 24.7g; Sugar: 14.2g; Sodium: 15000mg; Fiber: 0g

THANKSGIVING DINNER TURKEY

Serves: 16 | **Cooking Time:** 4 hours | **Prep Time:** 15 mins

INGREDIENTS:

- ½ lb. butter, softened
- 2 tbsp. fresh thyme, chopped
- 2 tbsp. fresh rosemary, chopped
- 6 garlic cloves, crushed
- 1 (20-lb.) whole turkey, neck and giblets removed
- Salt and freshly ground black pepper, to taste

INSTRUCTIONS:

1. Set the temperature of Traeger Grill to 300 degrees F and preheat with closed lid for 15 mins, using charcoal.
2. In a bowl, place butter, fresh herbs, garlic, salt and black pepper and mix well.
3. With your fingers, separate the turkey skin from breast to create a pocket.
4. Stuff the breast pocket with ¼-inch thick layer of butter mixture.
5. Season the turkey with salt and black pepper evenly.
6. Arrange the turkey onto the grill and cook for 3-4 hours.
7. Remove the turkey from grill and place onto a cutting board for about 15-20 mins before carving.
8. With a sharp knife, cut the turkey into desired-sized pieces and serve.

NUTRITION INFORMATION:

Calories per serving: 965; Carbohydrates: 0.6g; Protein: 106.5g; Fat: 52g; Sugar: 0g; Sodium: 1916mg; Fiber: 0.2g

PERFECTLY SMOKED TURKEY LEGS

Serves: 6 | **Cooking Time:** 4 hours | **Prep Time:** 15 mins

INGREDIENTS:

For Turkey:
- 3 tbsp. Worcestershire sauce
- 1 tbsp. canola oil
- 6 turkey legs

For Rub:
- ¼ C. chipotle seasoning
- 1 tbsp. brown sugar
- 1 tbsp. paprika

For Sauce:
- 1 C. white vinegar
- 1 tbsp. canola oil
- 1 tbsp. chipotle BBQ sauce

INSTRUCTIONS:

1. For turkey in a bowl, add the Worcestershire sauce and canola oil and mix well.
2. With your fingers, loosen the skin of legs.
3. With your fingers coat the legs under the skin with oil mixture.
4. In another bowl, mix together rub ingredients.
5. Rub the spice mixture under and outer surface of turkey legs generously.
6. Transfer the legs into a large sealable bag and refrigerate for about 2-4 hours.
7. Remove the turkey legs from refrigerator and set aside at room temperature for at least 30 mins before cooking.
8. Set the temperature of Traeger Grill to 200-220 degrees F and preheat with closed lid for 15 mins.
9. In a small pan, mix together all sauce ingredients on low heat and cook until warmed completely, stirring continuously.
10. Place the turkey legs onto the grill cook for about 3½-4 hours, coating with sauce after every 45 mins.
11. Serve hot.

NUTRITION INFORMATION:

Calories per serving: 430; Carbohydrates:
4.9g; Protein: 51.2g; Fat: 19.5g; Sugar: 3.9g;
Sodium: 1474mg; Fiber: 0.5g

AUTHENTIC HOLIDAY TURKEY BREAST

Serves: 6 | **Cooking Time:** 4 hours | **Prep Time:** 15 mins

INGREDIENTS:

- ½ C. honey
- ¼ C. dry sherry
- 1 tbsp. butter
- 2 tbsp. fresh lemon juice
- Salt, to taste
- 1 (3-3½-pound) skinless, boneless turkey breast

INSTRUCTIONS:

1. In a small pan, place honey, sherry and butter over low heat and cook until the mixture becomes smooth, stirring continuously.
2. Remove from heat and stir in lemon juice and salt. Set aside to cool.
3. Transfer the honey mixture and turkey breast in a sealable bag.
4. Seal the bag and shake to coat well.
5. Refrigerate for about 6-10 hours.
6. Set the temperature of Traeger Grill to 225-250 degrees F and preheat with closed lid for 15 mins.
7. Place the turkey breast onto the grill and cook for about 2½-4 hours or until desired doneness.
8. Remove turkey breast from grill and place onto a cutting board for about 15-20 mins before slicing.
9. With a sharp knife, cut the turkey breast into desired-sized slices and serve.

NUTRITION INFORMATION:

Calories per serving: 443; Carbohydrates: 23.7g; Protein: 59.2g; Fat: 11.4g; Sugar: 23.4g; Sodium: 138mg; Fiber: 0.1g

CHINESE INSPIRED DUCK LEGS

Serves: 8 | **Cooking Time:** 1 hour 10 mins | **Prep Time:** 15 mins

INGREDIENTS:

For Glaze:
- ¼ C. fresh orange juice
- ¼ C. orange marmalade
- ¼ C. mirin
- 2 tbsp. hoisin sauce
- ½ tsp. red pepper flakes, crushed

For Duck:
- 1 tsp. kosher salt
- ¾ tsp. freshly ground black pepper
- ¾ tsp. Chinese five-spice powder
- 8 (6-oz.) duck legs

INSTRUCTIONS:

1. Set the temperature of Traeger Grill to 235 degrees F and preheat with closed lid for 15 mins.
2. Forb glaze: in a small pan, add all ingredients over medium-high heat and bring to gentle boil, stirring continuously.
3. Remove from heat and set aside.
4. For rub: in a small bowl, mix together salt, black pepper and five-spice powder.
5. Rub the duck legs with spice rub evenly.
6. Place the duck legs onto the grill, skin side up and cook for about 50 mins.
7. Coat the duck legs with glaze ad cook for about 20 mins, flipping and coating with glaze after every 5 mins.

NUTRITION INFORMATION:

Calories per serving: 303; Carbohydrates: 0.1g; Protein: 49.5g; Fat: 10.2g; Sugar: 0g; Sodium: 474mg; Fiber: 0.1g

SUCCULENT DUCK BREAST

Serves: 4 | **Cooking Time:** 10 mins | **Prep Time:** 10 mins

INGREDIENTS:

- 4 (6-oz.) boneless duck breasts
- 2 tbsp. chicken rub

INSTRUCTIONS:

1. Set the temperature of Traeger Grill to 275 degrees F and preheat with closed lid for 15 mins.
2. With a sharp knife, score the skin of the duck into ¼-inch diamond pattern.
3. Season the duck breast with rub evenly.
4. Place the duck breasts onto the grill, meat side down and cook for about 10 mins.
5. Now, set the temperature of Traeger Grill to 400 degrees F.
6. Now, arrange the breasts, skin side down and cook for about 10 mins, flipping once halfway through.
7. Remove from the grill and serve.

NUTRITION INFORMATION:

Calories per serving: 231; Carbohydrates: 1.5g; Protein: 37.4g; Fat: 6.8g; Sugar: 0g; Sodium: 233mg; Fiber: 0g

CHRISTMAS DINNER GOOSE

Serves: 12 | **Cooking Time:** 3 hours | **Prep Time:** 20 mins

INGREDIENTS:

- 1½ C. kosher salt
- 1 C. brown sugar
- 20 C. water
- 1 (12-lb.) whole goose, giblets removed
- 1 naval orange, cut into 6 wedges
- 1 large onion, cut into 8 wedges
- 2 bay leaves
- ¼ C. juniper berries, crushed
- 12 black peppercorns
- Salt and freshly ground black pepper, to taste
- 1 apple, cut into 6 wedges
- 2-3 fresh parsley sprigs

INSTRUCTIONS:

1. Trim off any loose neck skin.
2. Then, trim the first two joints off the wings.
3. Wash the goose under cold running water and with paper towels, pat dry it.
4. With the tip of a paring knife, prick the goose all over the skin.
5. In a large pitcher, dissolve kosher salt and brown sugar in water.
6. Squeeze 3 orange wedges into brine.
7. Add goose, 4 onion wedges, bay leaves, juniper berries and peppercorns in brine and refrigerate for 24 hours.
8. Set the temperature of Traeger Grill to 350 degrees F and preheat with closed lid for 15 mins.
9. Remove the goose from brine and with paper towels, pat dry completely.
10. Season the in and outside of goose with salt and black pepper evenly.
11. Stuff the cavity with apple wedges, herbs, remaining orange and onion wedges.
12. With kitchen strings, tie the legs together loosely.
13. Place the goose onto a rack arranged in a shallow roasting pan.
14. Arrange the goose on grill and cook for about 1 hour.
15. With a basting bulb, remove some of the fat from the pan and cook for about 1 hour.
16. Again, remove excess fat from the pan and cook for about ½-1 hour more.
17. Remove goose from grill and place onto a cutting board for about 20 mins before carving.
18. With a sharp knife, cut the goose into desired-sized pieces and serve.

NUTRITION INFORMATION:

Calories per serving: 907; Carbohydrates: 23.5g; Protein: 5.6g; Fat: 60.3g; Sugar: 19.9g; Sodium: 8000mg; Fiber: 1.1g

FISH & SEAFOOD RECIPES

WINE INFUSED SALMON

Serves: 4 | **Cooking Time:** 5 hours | **Prep Time:** 15 mins

INGREDIENTS:

- 2 C. low-sodium soy sauce
- 1 C. dry white wine
- 1 C. water
- ½ tsp. Tabasco sauce
- 1/3 C. sugar
- ¼ C. salt
- ½ tsp. garlic powder
- ½ tsp. onion powder
- Freshly ground black pepper, to taste
- 4 (6-oz.) salmon fillets

INSTRUCTIONS:

1. In a large bowl, add all ingredients except salmon and stir until sugar is dissolved.
2. Add salmon fillets and coat with brine well.
3. Refrigerate, covered overnight.
4. Remove salmon from bowl and rinse under cold running water.
5. With paper towels, pat dry the salmon fillets.
6. Arrange a wire rack in a sheet pan.
7. Place the salmon fillets onto wire rack, skin side down and set aside to cool for about 1 hour.
8. Set the temperature of Traeger Grill to 165 degrees F and preheat with closed lid for 15 mins, using charcoal.
9. Place the salmon fillets onto the grill, skin side down and cook for about 3-5 hours or until desired doneness.
10. Remove the salmon fillets from grill and serve hot.

NUTRITION INFORMATION:

Calories per serving: 377; Carbohydrates: 26.3g; Protein: 41.1g; Fat: 10.5g; Sugar: 25.1g; Sodium: 14000mg; Fiber: 0g

CITRUS SALMON

Serves: 6 | **Cooking Time:** 30 mins | **Prep Time:** 15 mins

INGREDIENTS:

- 2 (1-lb.) salmon fillets
- Salt and freshly ground black pepper, to taste
- 1 tbsp. seafood seasoning
- 2 lemons, sliced
- 2 limes, sliced

INSTRUCTIONS:

1. Set the temperature of Traeger Grill to 225 degrees F and preheat with closed lid for 15 mins.
2. Season the salmon fillets with salt, black pepper and seafood seasoning evenly.
3. Place the salmon fillets onto the grill and top each with lemon and lime slices evenly.
4. Cook for about 30 mins.
5. Remove the salmon fillets from grill and serve hot.

NUTRITION INFORMATION:

Calories per serving: 327; Carbohydrates: 1g; Protein: 36.1g; Fat: 19.8g; Sugar: 0.2g; Sodium: 237mg; Fiber: 0.3g

OMEGA-3 RICH SALMON

Serves: 6 | **Cooking Time:** 20 mins | **Prep Time:** 15 mins

INGREDIENTS:

- 6 (6-oz.) skinless salmon fillets
- 1/3 C. olive oil
- ¼ C. spice rub
- ¼ C. honey
- 2 tbsp. Sriracha
- 2 tbsp. fresh lime juice

INSTRUCTIONS:

1. Set the temperature of Traeger Grill to 300 degrees F and preheat with closed lid for 15 mins.
2. Coat salmon fillets with olive oil and season with rub evenly.
3. In a small bowl, mix together remaining ingredients.
4. Arrange salmon fillets onto the grill, flat-side up and cook for about 7-10 mins per side, coating with honey mixture once halfway through.
5. Serve hot alongside remaining honey mixture.

NUTRITION INFORMATION:

Calories per serving: 384; Carbohydrates: 15.7g; Protein: 33g; Fat: 21.7g; Sugar: 11.6g; Sodium: 621mg; Fiber: 0g

ENTICING MAHI-MAHI

Serves: 4 | **Cooking Time:** 10 mins | **Prep Time:** 10 mins

INGREDIENTS:

- 4 (6-oz.) mahi-mahi fillets
- 2 tbsp. olive oil
- Salt and freshly ground black pepper, to taste

INSTRUCTIONS:

1. Set the temperature of Traeger Grill to 350 degrees F and preheat with closed lid for 15 mins.
2. Coat fish fillets with olive oil and season with salt and black pepper evenly.
3. Place the fish fillets onto the grill and cook for about 5 mins per side.
4. Remove the fish fillets from grill and serve hot.

NUTRITION INFORMATION:

Calories per serving: 195; Carbohydrates: 0g; Protein: 31.6g; Fat: 7g; Sugar: 0g; Sodium: 182mg; Fiber: 0g

SUPER-TASTY TROUT

Serves: 8 | **Cooking Time:** 5 hours | **Prep Time:** 15 mins

INGREDIENTS:

- 1 (7-lb.) whole lake trout, butterflied
- ½ C. kosher salt
- ½ C. fresh rosemary, chopped
- 2 tsp. lemon zest, grated finely

INSTRUCTIONS:

1. Rub the trout with salt generously and then, sprinkle with rosemary and lemon zest.
2. Arrange the trout in a large baking dish and refrigerate for about 7-8 hours.
3. Remove the trout from baking dish and rinse under cold running water to remove the salt.
4. With paper towels, pat dry the trout completely.
5. Arrange a wire rack in a sheet pan.
6. Place the trout onto the wire rack, skin side down and refrigerate for about 24 hours.
7. Set the temperature of Traeger Grill to 180 degrees F and preheat with closed lid for 15 mins, using charcoal.
8. Place the trout onto the grill and cook for about 2-4 hours or until desired doneness.
9. Remove the trout from grill and place onto a cutting board for about 5 mins before serving.

NUTRITION INFORMATION:

Calories per serving: 633; Carbohydrates: 2.4g; Protein: 85.2g; Fat: 31.8g; Sugar: 0g; Sodium: 5000mg; Fiber: 1.6g

NO-FUSS TUNA BURGERS

Serves: 6 | **Cooking Time:** 15 mins | **Prep Time:** 15 mins

INGREDIENTS:

- 2 lb. tuna steak
- 1 green bell pepper, seeded and chopped
- 1 white onion, chopped
- 2 eggs
- 1 tsp. soy sauce
- 1 tbsp. blackened Saskatchewan rub
- Salt and freshly ground black pepper, to taste

INSTRUCTIONS:

1. Set the temperature of Traeger Grill to 500 degrees F and preheat with closed lid for 15 mins.
2. In a bowl, add all the ingredients and mix until well combined.
3. With greased hands, make patties from mixture.
4. Place the patties onto the grill close to the edges and cook for about 10-15 mins, flipping once halfway through.
5. Serve hot.

NUTRITION INFORMATION:

Calories per serving: 313; Carbohydrates: 3.4g; Protein: 47.5g; Fat: 11g; Sugar: 1.9g; Sodium: 174mg; Fiber: 0.7g

LIVELY FLAVORED SHRIMP

Serves: 6 | **Cooking Time:** 30 mins | **Prep Time:** 15 mins

INGREDIENTS:

- 8 oz. salted butter, melted
- ¼ C. Worcestershire sauce
- ¼ C. fresh parsley, chopped
- 1 lemon, quartered
- 2 lb. jumbo shrimp, peeled and deveined
- 3 tbsp. BBQ rub

INSTRUCTIONS:

1. In a metal baking pan, add all ingredients except for shrimp and BBQ rub and mix well.
2. Season the shrimp with BBQ rub evenly.
3. Add the shrimp in the pan with butter mixture and coat well.
4. Set aside for about 20-30 mins.
5. Set the temperature of Traeger Grill to 250 degrees F and preheat with closed lid for 15 mins.
6. Place the pan onto the grill and cook for about 25-30 mins.
7. Remove the pan from grill and serve hot.

NUTRITION INFORMATION:

Calories per serving: 462; Carbohydrates: 4.7g; Protein: 34.9g; Fat: 33.3g; Sugar: 2.1g; Sodium: 485mg; Fiber: 0.2g

FLAVOR-BURSTING PRAWN SKEWERS

Serves: 5 | **Cooking Time:** 8 mins | **Prep Time:** 15 mins

INGREDIENTS:

- ¼ C. fresh parsley leaves, minced
- 1 tbsp. garlic, crushed
- 2½ tbsp. olive oil
- 2 tbsp. Thai chili sauce
- 1 tbsp. fresh lime juice
- 1½ pounds prawns, peeled and deveined

INSTRUCTIONS:

1. In a large bowl, add all ingredients except for prawns and mix well.
2. In a resealable plastic bag, add marinade and prawns.
3. Seal the bag and shake to coat well
4. Refrigerate for about 20-30 mins.
5. Set the temperature of Traeger Grill to 450 degrees F and preheat with closed lid for 15 mins.
6. Remove the prawns from marinade and thread onto metal skewers.
7. Arrange the skewers onto the grill and cook for about 4 mins per side.
8. Remove the skewers from grill and serve hot.

NUTRITION INFORMATION:

Calories per serving: 234; Carbohydrates: 4.9g; Protein: 31.2g; Fat: 9.3g; Sugar: 1.7g; Sodium: 562mg; Fiber: 0.1g

YUMMY BUTTERY CLAMS

Serves: 6 | **Cooking Time:** 8 mins | **Prep Time:** 15 mins

INGREDIENTS:

- 24 littleneck clams
- ½ C. cold butter, chopped
- 2 tbsp. fresh parsley, minced
- 3 garlic cloves, minced
- 1 tsp. fresh lemon juice

INSTRUCTIONS:

1. Set the temperature of Traeger Grill to 450 degrees F and preheat with closed lid for 15 mins.
2. Scrub the clams under cold running water.
3. In a large casserole dish, mix together remaining ingredients.
4. Place the casserole dish onto the grill.
5. Now, arrange the clams directly onto the grill and cook for about 5-8 mins or until they are opened. (Discard any that fail to open).
6. With tongs, carefully transfer the opened clams into the casserole dish and remove from grill.
7. Serve immediately.

NUTRITION INFORMATION:

Calories per serving: 306; Carbohydrates: 6.4g; Protein: 29.3g; Fat: 7.6g; Sugar: 0.1g; Sodium: 237mg; Fiber: 0.1g

CRAZY DELICIOUS LOBSTER TAILS

Serves: 4 | **Cooking Time:** 25 mins | **Prep Time:** 15 mins

INGREDIENTS:

- ½ C. butter, melted
- 2 garlic cloves, minced
- 2 tsp. fresh lemon juice
- Salt and freshly ground black pepper, to taste
- 4 (8-oz.) lobster tails

INSTRUCTIONS:

1. Set the temperature of Traeger Grill to 450 degrees F and preheat with closed lid for 15 mins.
2. In a metal pan, add all ingredients except for lobster tails and mix well.
3. Place the pan onto the grill and cook for about 10 mins.
4. Meanwhile, cut down the top of the shell and expose lobster meat.
5. Remove pan of butter mixture from grill.
6. Coat the lobster meat with butter mixture.
7. Place the lobster tails onto the grill and cook for about 15 mins, coating with butter mixture once halfway through.
8. Remove from grill and serve hot.

NUTRITION INFORMATION:

Calories per serving: 409; Carbohydrates: 0.6g; Protein: 43.5g; Fat: 24.9g; Sugar: 0.1g; Sodium: 1305mg; Fiber: 0g

EXTRA RECIPES

SUMMER TREAT CORN

Serves: 6 | **Cooking Time:** 20 mins | **Prep Time:** 10 mins

INGREDIENTS:

- 6 fresh whole corn on the cob
- ½ C. butter
- Salt, to taste

INSTRUCTIONS:

1. Set the temperature of Traeger Grill to 400 degrees F and preheat with closed lid for 15 mins.
2. Husk the corn and remove all the silk.
3. Brush each corn with melted butter and sprinkle with salt.
4. Place the corn onto the grill and cook for about 20 mins, rotating after every 5 mins and brushing with butter once halfway through.
5. Serve warm.

NUTRITION INFORMATION:

Calories per serving: 334; Carbohydrates: 43.5g; Protein: 7.7g; Fat: 18.1g; Sugar: 7.5g; Sodium: 171mg; Fiber: 6.3g

CRUNCHY POTATO WEDGES

Serves: 5 | **Cooking Time:** 16 mins | **Prep Time:** 15 mins

INGREDIENTS:

- 4 Yukon gold potatoes
- 2 tbsp. olive oil
- 1 tbsp. garlic, minced
- 2 tsp. onion powder
- ½ tsp. red pepper flakes, crushed
- Salt and freshly ground black pepper, to taste

INSTRUCTIONS:

1. Set the temperature of Traeger Grill to 500 degrees F and preheat with closed lid for 15 mins.
2. Cut each potato into 8 equal-sized wedges.
3. In a large bowl, add potato wedges and remaining ingredients and toss to coat well.
4. Arrange the potato wedges onto the grill and cook for about 8 mins per side.
5. Remove from grill and serve hot.

NUTRITION INFORMATION:

Calories per serving: 157; Carbohydrates: 25.7g; Protein: 3g; Fat: 5.8g; Sugar: 1.3g; Sodium: 46mg; Fiber: 2g

TWICE GRILLED POTATOES

Serves: 6 | **Cooking Time:** 4 hours | **Prep Time:** 20 mins

INGREDIENTS:

- 6 russet potatoes
- 2 tbsp. olive oil
- Salt, to taste
- 8 cooked bacon slices, crumbled
- ½ C. heavy whipping cream
- 4 oz. cream cheese, softened
- 4 tbsp. butter, softened
- 4 jalapeño peppers, seeded and chopped
- 1 tsp. seasoned salt
- 2 C. Monterrey Jack cheese, grated and divided

INSTRUCTIONS:

1. Set the temperature of Traeger Grill to 225 degrees F and preheat with closed lid for 15 mins.
2. With paper towels, pat dry the washed potatoes completely.
3. Coat the potatoes with olive oil sprinkle with some salt.
4. Arrange potatoes onto the grill and cook for about 3-3½ hours.
5. Remove the potatoes from grill and cut them in half lengthwise.
6. With a large spoon carefully, scoop out the potato flesh from skins, leaving a little potato layer.
7. In a large bowl, add potato flesh and mash it slightly.
8. Add bacon, cream, cream cheese, butter, jalapeno, seasoned salt and 1 C. of Monterrey Jack cheese and gently, stir to combine.
9. Stuff the potato skins with bacon mixture and top with remaining Monterrey Jack cheese.
10. Arrange the stuffed potatoes onto a baking sheet.
11. Place the baking sheet in grill and cook for about 30 mins.
12. Serve hot.

NUTRITION INFORMATION:

Calories per serving: 539; Carbohydrates: 35.7g; Protein: 17.6g; Fat: 37g; Sugar: 2.8g; Sodium: 1355mg; Fiber: 5.5g

MOUTHWATERING CAULIFLOWER

Serves: 8 | **Cooking Time:** 30 mins | **Prep Time:** 15 mins

INGREDIENTS:

- 2 large heads cauliflower head, stem removed and cut into 2-inch florets
- 3 tbsp. olive oil
- Salt and freshly ground black pepper, to taste
- ¼ C. fresh parsley, chopped finely

INSTRUCTIONS:

1. Set the temperature of Traeger Grill to 500 degrees F and preheat with closed lid for 15 mins.
2. In a large bowl, add cauliflower florets, oil, salt and black pepper and toss to coat well.
3. Divide the cauliflower florets onto 2 baking sheets and spread in an even layer.
4. Place the baking sheets onto the grill and cook for about 20-30 mins, stirring once after 15 mins.
5. Remove the vegetables from grill and transfer into a large bowl.
6. Immediately, add the parsley and toss to coat well.
7. Serve immediately.

NUTRITION INFORMATION:

Calories per serving: 62; Carbohydrates: 3.6g; Protein: 1.4g; Fat: 5.3g; Sugar: 1.6g; Sodium: 40mg; Fiber: 1.7g

SUPER-ADDICTING MUSHROOMS

Serves: 4 | **Cooking Time:** 45 mins | **Prep Time:** 15 mins

INGREDIENTS:

- 4 C. fresh whole baby Portobello mushrooms, cleaned
- 1 tbsp. canola oil
- 1 tsp. granulated garlic
- 1 tsp. onion powder
- Salt and freshly ground black pepper, to taste

INSTRUCTIONS:

1. Set the temperature of Traeger Grill to 180 degrees F and preheat with closed lid for 15 mins, using charcoal.
2. In a bowl, add all ingredients and mix well.
3. Place the mushrooms onto the grill and cook for about 30 mins.
4. Remove the mushrooms from grill.
5. Now, preheat the Grill to 400 degrees F and preheat with closed lid for 15 mins.
6. Place the mushrooms onto the grill and cook for about 15 mins.
7. Remove the mushrooms from grill and serve warm.

NUTRITION INFORMATION:

Calories per serving: 50; Carbohydrates: 3.3g; Protein: 2.4g; Fat: 3.7g; Sugar: 1.6g; Sodium: 43mg; Fiber: 0.8g

VEGGIE LOVER'S BURGERS

Serves: 6 | **Cooking Time:** 51 mins | **Prep Time:** 20 mins

INGREDIENTS:

- ¾ C. lentils
- 1 tbsp. ground flaxseed
- 2 tbsp. extra-virgin olive oil
- 1 onion, chopped
- 2 garlic cloves, minced
- Salt and freshly ground black pepper, to taste
- 1 C. walnuts, toasted
- ¾ C. breadcrumbs
- 1 tsp. ground cumin
- 1 tsp. paprika

INSTRUCTIONS:

1. In a pan of boiling water, add the lentils and cook for about 15 mins or until soft.
2. Drain the lentils completely and set aside.
3. In a small bowl, mix together the flaxseed with 4 tbsp. of water. Set aside for about 5 mins.
4. In a medium skillet, heat the oil over medium heat and sauté the onion for about 4-6 mins.
5. Add the garlic and a pinch of salt and pepper and sauté for about 30 seconds.
6. Remove from the heat and place the onion mixture into a food processor.
7. Add the ¾ of the lentils, flaxseed mixture, walnuts, breadcrumbs and spices and pulse until smooth.
8. Transfer the mixture into a bowl and gently, fold in the remaining lentils.
9. Make 6 patties from the mixture.
10. Place the patties onto a parchment paper-lined plate and refrigerate for at least 30 mins.
11. Set the temperature of Traeger Grill to 425 degrees F and preheat with closed lid for 15 mins, using charcoal.
12. Place the burgers onto the grill and cook for about 8-10 mins flipping once halfway through.
13. Serve hot.

NUTRITION INFORMATION:

Calories per serving: 324; Carbohydrates: 28.9g; Protein: 13.6g; Fat: 18.5g; Sugar: 13.6g; Sodium: 130mg; Fiber: 10.3g

SATISFYING VEGGIE CASSEROLE

Serves: 10 | **Cooking Time:** 3 hours | **Prep Time:** 15 mins

INGREDIENTS:

- 5 tbsp. olive oil, divided
- 6 C. onions, sliced thinly
- 1 tbsp. fresh thyme, chopped and divided
- Salt and freshly ground black pepper, to taste
- 1 tbsp. unsalted butter
- 1¼ lb. Yukon gold potatoes, peeled and 1/8-inch thick slices
- ½ C. heavy cream
- 2¼ lb. tomatoes, cut into ¼-inch thick slices
- ¼ cup black olives, pitted and sliced

INSTRUCTIONS:

1. In a large cast iron pan, heat 3 tbsp. of oil and over high heat and cook onions, 1 tsp. of thyme, salt and black pepper for about 5 mins, stirring occasionally.
2. Add the butter and cook over medium heat for about 15 mins.
3. Reduce the heat to low and cook for about 10 mins.
4. Set the temperature of Traeger Grill to 350 degrees F and preheat with closed lid for 15 mins.
5. Meanwhile, in a bowl, add potatoes slices, cream, 1 tsp. of thyme, salt and black pepper and toss to coat.
6. In another bowl, add tomato slices, salt and black pepper and toss to coat.
7. Transfer half of the caramelized onions into a small bowl.
8. In the bottom of the cast iron pan, spread the remaining onion slices evenly and top with 1 layer of potatoes and tomatoes.
9. Drizzle with 2 tbsp. of cream from potato mixture and 1 tbsp. of olive oil.
10. Sprinkle with a little salt, black pepper and ½ tsp. of thyme.
11. Spread remaining caramelized onions on top, followed by potatoes, tomatoes and olives.
12. Drizzle with remaining cream from the potatoes and remaining tbsp. of olive oil.
13. Sprinkle with a little salt, black pepper and remaining ½ tsp. of thyme.
14. With a piece of foil, cover the cast iron pan tightly.
15. Place the pan onto the grill and cook for about 2 hours.
16. Remove from grill and uncover the cast iron pan.
17. Now, set the temperature of Traeger Grill to 450 degrees F.
18. Place the cast iron pan, uncovered onto the grill and cook for about 25-30 mins.
19. Remove from grill and serve hot.

NUTRITION INFORMATION:

Calories per serving: 158; Carbohydrates: 14.8g; Protein: 2.3g; Fat: 11.1g; Sugar: 5.8g; Sodium: 65mg; Fiber: 3.2g

NORTH AMERICAN POT PIE

Serves: 10 | **Cooking Time:** 1 hour 25 mins | **Prep Time:** 15 mins

INGREDIENTS:

- 2 tbsp. cornstarch
- 2 tbsp. water
- 3 C. chicken broth
- 1 C. milk
- 3 tbsp. butter
- 1 tbsp. fresh rosemary, chopped
- 1 tbsp. fresh thyme, chopped
- Salt and freshly ground black pepper, to taste
- 2¾ C. frozen chopped broccoli, thawed
- 3 C. frozen peas, thawed
- 3 C. chopped frozen carrots, thawed
- 1 frozen puff pastry sheet

INSTRUCTIONS:

1. Set the temperature of Traeger Grill to 375 degrees F and preheat with closed lid for 15 mins.
2. In a small bowl, dissolve cornstarch in water. Set aside.
3. In a pan, add broth, milk, butter and herbs over medium heat and bring to a boil.
4. Add the cornstarch mixture and stir to combine well.
5. Stir in salt and black pepper and remove from the heat.
6. In a large bowl, add the vegetables and milk sauce and mix well.
7. Transfer mixture into a cast iron skillet.
8. With the puff pastry, cover the mixture and cut excess from edges.
9. Place the skillet onto the grill and cook for about 80 mins.
10. Remove the pan from grill and set aside for about 15 mins before serving.
11. Cut the pie into desired-sized portions and serve.

NUTRITION INFORMATION:

Calories per serving: 257; Carbohydrates: 26.1g; Protein: 7.6g; Fat: 14g; Sugar: 5.8g; Sodium: 408mg; Fiber: 4.7g

POTLUCK FAVORITE BAKED BEANS

Serves: 10 | **Cooking Time:** 3 hours 5 mins | **Prep Time:** 15 mins

INGREDIENTS:

- 1 tbsp. butter
- ½ of red bell pepper, seeded and chopped
- ½ of medium onion, chopped
- 2 jalapeño peppers, chopped
- 2 (28-oz.) cans baked beans, rinsed and drained
- 8 oz. pineapple chunks, drained
- 1 C. BBQ sauce
- 1 C. brown sugar
- 1 tbsp. ground mustard

INSTRUCTIONS:

1. Set the temperature of Traeger Grill to 220-250 degrees F and preheat with closed lid for 15 mins.
2. In a non-stick skillet, melt butter over medium heat and sauté the bell peppers, onion and jalapeño peppers for about 4-5 mins.
3. Remove from heat and transfer the pepper mixture into a bowl.
4. Add remaining ingredients and stir to combine.
5. Transfer the mixture into a Dutch oven.
6. Place the Dutch oven onto the grill and cook for about 2½-3 hours.
7. Remove from grill and serve hot.

NUTRITION INFORMATION:

Calories per serving: 364; Carbohydrates: 61.4g; Protein: 9.4g; Fat: 9.8g; Sugar: 23.5g; Sodium: 1036mg; Fiber: 9.7g

TRADITIONAL ENGLISH MAC N' CHEESE

Serves: 12 | **Cooking Time:** 1 hour 20 mins | **Prep Time:** 15 mins

INGREDIENTS:

- 2 lb. elbow macaroni
- ¾ C. butter
- ½ C. flour
- 1 tsp. dry mustard
- 1½ C. milk
- 2 lb. Velveeta cheese, cut into ½-inch cubes
- Salt and freshly ground black pepper, to taste
- 1½ C. cheddar cheese, shredded
- 2 C. plain dry breadcrumbs
- Paprika, to taste

INSTRUCTIONS:

1. Set the temperature of Traeger Grill to 350 degrees F and preheat with closed lid for 15 mins.
2. In a large pan of lightly salted boiling water, cook the macaroni for about 7-8 mins.
3. Drain the macaroni well and transfer into a large bowl.
4. Meanwhile, in a medium pan, melt 8 tbsp. of butter over medium heat.
5. Slowly, add flour and mustard, beating continuously until smooth.
6. Cook for about 2 mins, beating continuously.
7. Slowly, add milk, beating continuously until smooth.
8. Reduce the heat to medium-low and slowly, stir in Velveeta cheese until melted.
9. Stir in salt and black pepper and remove from heat.
10. Place cheese sauce over cooked macaroni and gently, stir to combine.
11. Place the macaroni mixture into greased casserole dish evenly and sprinkle with cheddar cheese.
12. In a small frying pan, melt remaining 4 tbsp. of butter.
13. Stir in breadcrumbs and remove from heat.
14. Place breadcrumbs mixture over cheddar cheese evenly and sprinkle with paprika lightly.
15. Arrange the casserole dish onto the grill and cook for about 45-60 mins, rotating the pan once halfway through.
16. Serve hot.

NUTRITION INFORMATION:

Calories per serving: 914; Carbohydrates: 99.9g; Protein: 37.2g; Fat: 42.3g; Sugar: 12g; Sodium: 1600mg; Fiber: 4.1g

AMAZING IRISH SODA BREAD

Serves: 10 | **Cooking Time:** 1½ hours | **Prep Time:** 15 mins

INGREDIENTS:

- 4 C. flour
- 1 C. raisins
- ½ C. sugar
- 1 tbsp. caraway seeds
- 2 tsp. baking powder
- 1 tsp. baking soda
- ¾ tsp. salt
- 1¼ C. buttermilk
- 1 C. sour cream
- 2 eggs

INSTRUCTIONS:

1. Set the temperature of Traeger Grill to 350 degrees F and preheat with closed lid for 15 mins.
2. Grease a 9-inch round cake pan.
3. Reserve 1 tbsp. of flour in a bowl.
4. In a large bowl, mix together remaining flour, raisins, sugar, caraway seeds, baking powder, baking soda and salt.
5. In another small bowl, add buttermilk, sour cream and eggs and beat until well combined.
6. Add egg mixture into flour mixture and mix until just moistened.
7. With your hands, knead the dough until sticky.
8. Place the dough into the prepared pan evenly and cut a 4x¾-inch deep slit in the top.
9. Dust the top with reserved flour.
10. Place the pan onto the grill and cook for about 1½ hours or until a toothpick inserted in the center comes out clean.
11. Remove from grill and place the pan onto a wire rack to cool for about 10 mins.
12. Carefully, invert the bread onto the wire rack to cool completely before slicing.
13. Cut the bread into desired-sized slices and sere.

NUTRITION INFORMATION:

Calories per serving: 340; Carbohydrates: 63g; Protein: 8.6g; Fat: 6.6g; Sugar: 20.3g; Sodium: 361mg; Fiber: 2.2g

NATIVE SOUTHERN CORNBREAD

Serves: 8 | **Cooking Time:** 20 mins | **Prep Time:** 15 mins

INGREDIENTS:

- 2 tbsp. butter
- 1½ C. all-purpose flour
- 1½ C. yellow cornmeal
- 2 tbsp. sugar
- 3 tsp. baking powder
- ¾ tsp. baking soda
- ¾ tsp. salt
- 1 C. whole milk
- 1 C. buttermilk
- 3 large eggs
- 3 tbsp. butter, melted

INSTRUCTIONS:

1. Set the temperature of Traeger Grill to 400 degrees F and preheat with closed lid for 15 mins.
2. In a 13x9-inch baking dish, place 2 tbsp. of butter.
3. Place the baking dish onto grill to melt butter and heat up the pan.
4. In a large bowl, mix together flour, cornmeal, sugar, baking powder, baking soda and salt.
5. In another bowl, add milk, buttermilk, eggs and melted butter and beat until well combined.
6. Add the egg mixture into flour mixture and mix until just moistened.
7. Carefully, remove the heated baking dish from grill.
8. Place the bread mixture into heated baking dish evenly.
9. Place the pan onto the grill and cook for about 20 mins or until a toothpick inserted in the center comes out clean.
10. Remove from grill and place the pan onto a wire rack to cool for about 10 mins.
11. Carefully, invert the bread onto the wire rack to cool completely before slicing.
12. Cut the bread into desired-sized slices and sere.

NUTRITION INFORMATION:

Calories per serving: 302; Carbohydrates: 42.4g; Protein: 8.7g; Fat: 10.4g; Sugar: 6.4g; Sodium: 467mg; Fiber: 2.3g

DECADENT CHOCOLATE CHEESECAKE

Serves: 8 | **Cooking Time:** 1 hour 10 mins | **Prep Time:** 20 mins

INGREDIENTS:

For Base:

- 1 C. chocolate wafer crumbs
- 2 tbsp. butter, melted

For Filling:

- 4 oz. unsweetened baking chocolate, chopped
- 16 oz. cream cheese, softened
- ¾ C. white sugar
- 2 eggs
- 1 tsp. vanilla extract

For Topping:

- ¼ C. heavy cream
- 2 oz. unsweetened baking chocolate, chopped finely
- ¼ C. white sugar
- 1 tbsp. unsalted butter

INSTRUCTIONS:

1. Set the temperature of Traeger Grill to 325 degrees F and preheat with closed lid for 15 mins.
2. For base: in a bowl, mix together wafer crumbs and melted butter.
3. Line an 8-inch springform pan with parchment paper.
4. Place the crumb mixture in the bottom of prepared springform pan and gently, press to fit.
5. Place the pan onto the grill and cook for about 10 mins.
6. Remove the pan from grill and set aside to cool.
7. For filling: in a microwave-safe bowl, add chocolate and microwave on High for about 1-2 mins or until melted, stirring after every 30 seconds.
8. Remove from microwave and set aside to cool slightly.
9. In another bowl, add cream cheese and sugar and beat until light and fluffy.
10. Add the eggs, one at a time, beating well after each addition.
11. Add melted chocolate and vanilla extract and mix well.
12. Place filling mixture over cooled base evenly and cook onto the grill for about 45-50 mins.
13. Remove the cheesecake from grill and place onto a wire rack to cool.
14. For topping: in a heavy-bottomed pan, place heavy cream over medium-low heat and cook until heated through.
15. Add chocolate, sugar and butter and cook until sugar dissolves, stirring continuously.
16. Remove the pan from heat and set aside to cool slightly.
17. Pour chocolate mixture over the cooled cheesecake evenly.
18. Refrigerate for at least 4 hours before serving.

NUTRITION INFORMATION:

Calories per serving: 489; Carbohydrates: 43.2g; Protein: 9.4g; Fat: 35.4g; Sugar: 29.6g; Sodium: 271mg; Fiber: 4g

SWEET TOOTH CARVING RHUBARB CRUNCH

Serves: 8 | **Cooking Time:** 1 hour | **Prep Time:** 15 mins

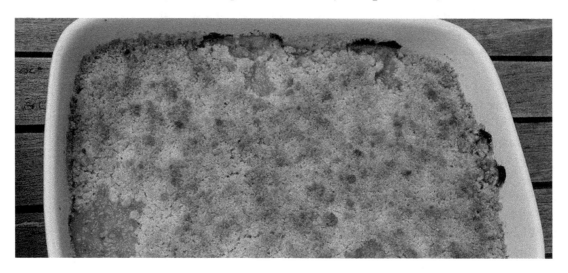

INGREDIENTS:

- 1 C. oatmeal
- 1 C. flour
- 1 C. brown sugar
- ½ C. butter, melted
- ¼ tsp. salt
- 4 C. raw rhubarb, chopped finely
- 1 C. white sugar
- 2 tbsp. cornstarch
- 1 C. cold water
- 1 tsp. vanilla extract

INSTRUCTIONS:

1. Set the temperature of Traeger Grill to 350 degrees F and preheat with closed lid for 15 mins.
2. In a bowl, add oatmeal, flour, brown sugar, butter and salt and mix until well combined.
3. In a pan, add white sugar, cornstarch, cold water and vanilla extract and cook until sugar is dissolves, stirring continuously.
4. Place half of the four mixture into a 9x12-inch pan and top with chopped rhubarb evenly.
5. Place sugar mixture over rhubarb evenly and top with remaining flour mixture.
6. Place the pan onto the grill and cook for about 1 hour.
7. Remove from grill and place the crunch onto a wire rack to cool in the pan for about 10 mins.
8. Cut into desired-sized slices and serve warm.

NUTRITION INFORMATION:

Calories per serving: 382; Carbohydrates: 66.3g; Protein: 3.7g; Fat: 12.5g; Sugar: 43.5g; Sodium: 164mg; Fiber: 2.6g

FALL SEASON APPLE PIE

Serves: 8 | **Cooking Time:** 1 hour | **Prep Time:** 15 mins

INGREDIENTS:

- 8 C. apples, peeled, cored and sliced thinly
- ¾ C. sugar
- 1 tbsp. fresh lemon juice
- 1 tsp. ground cinnamon
- ¼ tsp. ground nutmeg
- 2 whole frozen pie crusts, thawed
- ¼ C. apple jelly
- 2 tbsp. apple juice
- 2 tbsp. heavy whipping cream

INSTRUCTIONS:

1. Set the temperature of Traeger Grill to 375 degrees F and preheat with closed lid for 15 mins.
2. In a bowl, add the apples, sugar, lemon juice, flour, cinnamon, and nutmeg and mix well.
3. Roll the pie crust dough into two (11-inch) circles.
4. Arrange 1 dough circle into a 9-inch pie plate.
5. Spread the apple jelly over dough evenly and top with apple mixture.
6. Dampen the edges of dough crust with apple juice.
7. Cover with the top crust, pressing the edges together to seal.
8. Trim the pastry, and flute the edges.
9. With a sparing knife, make several small slits in the top crust.
10. Brush the top of the pie with the cream.
11. Place the pie pan onto the grill and cook for about 50-60 mins.
12. Remove from the grill and place the pie onto a wire rack to cool slightly.
13. Serve warm.

NUTRITION INFORMATION:

Calories per serving: 419; Carbohydrates: 79.5g; Protein: 2.2g; Fat: 12.3g; Sugar: 54.2g; Sodium: 214mg; Fiber: 6.1g

CPSIA information can be obtained
at www.ICGtesting.com
Printed in the USA
LVHW060258191020
669130LV00010B/385